To Carl,
All the best in your
retirement, enjoy the
sports.

Peter Webb.
2000 ?

Published by

GENERAL STORE
PUBLISHING HOUSE INC.

1 Main St., Burnstown, Ontario, Canada K0J 1G0
(613) 432-7697

ISBN 0-919431-36-4

Printed and bound in Canada

DFR Printing, Pembroke, Ontario

Photography reproductions by Chromascan, Ottawa, Ontario

Designed by Bill Slavin and Marlene Barker

Copyright © 1987

General Store Publishing House Inc.

1 Main St., Burnstown, Ontario, Canada K0J 1G0

Canadian Cataloguing in Publication Data

Evans, Steve, 1955 -
        Heart and soul

ISBN 0-919431-36-4

1. Ottawa River Valley (Quebec and Ont.) –
Portraits. 2. Ottawa River Valley (Quebec and Ont.) –
Interviews. 3. Ottawa River Valley (Quebec and
Ont.) – Biography. I. Title.

FC2775.1.A1E93 1987   971.3'8'0092   C87-090331-4

First Printing October 1987   Second Printing May 1992

HEART & SOUL

PORTRAITS OF CANADA'S OTTAWA VALLEY

Steve Evans

This book is dedicated to Teresa.
Thanks for all your
help and encouragement
through the two years it took
tu complete this book.

A Word of Thanks

A special thanks to the people who helped me put this book together. To Tim Gordon, my publisher, who liked my ideas and work enough to publish them. To Bill Slavin and Marlene Barker for all their help in producing the book. To editors Barbara Sibbald, Nancy Roach and Vicki Racey. To the staff of newspapers throughout the Ottawa Valley who helped me to find some of the people. Thanks to Jim Gauvreau for the use of his enlarger. Thanks to John Mellencamp for writing the song. Many thanks to the people who are in this book because without their trust and openness it wouldn't have been possible. And finally a special thank you to Bill and Pat Evans, my parents.

Foreword

When I sat down to write the introduction to this book I had a lot of trouble deciding what to write. I spent a few weeks making notes but everything sounded contrived. It just didn't reflect how I truly feel about this collection of photographs and interviews. I began to think back over the past two years and the time I had spent travelling through the Ottawa Valley and meeting people. The one thing I remember most of all is the song "Small Town". I'd heard it hundreds of times during my travels and I realized it reflected the Valley and the people who live there, young and old.

I was born and raised in the Ottawa Valley, a terrific area whose people have retained a strong sense of history and a unique spirit. Two years ago I decided I wanted to document the lives of some of these older people, not just in my town but throughout the Ottawa Valley. I wanted to hear about and share their adventures, their sorrows and triumphs.

Most of the people in these portraits could be your neighbours in the Valley. They're not famous, they're just nice people, interesting and very human. Most of all they are people with a story to tell, a story which is reflected as much in their faces and as it is in their words. I brought my studio equipment into their homes so I could capture them in their own surroundings. The words which accompany each picture are excerpts from interviews. I didn't write this book, they did. I wanted it to be as if you had just walked into their home and were talking to them. My hope is that you will be able to meet these people the way I did.

In a very real sense these portraits are part of me as well. I got a lot of memories tied up in this book. This is small town.

Small Town

Well I was born in a small town
And I live in a small town
Prob'ly die in a small town
Oh, those small communities

All my friends are so small town
My parents live in the same small
town
My job is so small town
Provides little opportunity

Educated in a small town
Taught the fear of Jesus in a
small town
Use to daydream in that small
town
Another boring romantic that's
me

But I've seen it all in a small town
Had myself a ball in a small town
Married an L.A. doll and brought
her to this small town
Now she's small town just like me

No I cannot forget where it is that
I come from
I cannot forget the people who
really love me
Yeah, I can be myself here in this
small town
And people let me be just what I
want to be

Got nothing against a big town
Still hayseed enough to say
Look who's in the big town
But my bed is in a small town
Oh, and that's good enough for
me

Well I was born in a small town
And I can breathe in a small town
Gonna die in this small town
And that's prob'ly where they'll
bury me

—John Mellencamp

Heart & Soul

Portraits of Canada's Ottawa Valley

Bill Dodge
General Store Keeper
Calabogie

This store is a little over a 100 years old. It was a man he started it, a man by the name of Mr. Bradey. He started it just on the road with a packsack selling jewelry and other things, with a horse and buggy, or a horse and sleigh. He kept that up for two or three years and then he built this. This is a good building, it keeps the heat and it is as straight as can be, no problems with the door or nothing. You can look at it from the edge and it is as straight as a line. I've been here for about 26 years. Never married, no. I'm over 50. It's hard to believe I was born March the eighth, 1904. I was born in Black Donald, just a little ways from here. I started to work when I was young, I was just 16. We built, oh, old barns in New Liskeard, the experimental farms there. A lot of people are kicking about the times now, but they have nothing to kick about, everybody has everything they want. They don't know what tough times are now. I lost my dog, my good one, oh from the rabid fox, but I got my little Rex, he's in the kitchen, he'll soon be a year old. I named all my dogs Rex, I had two or three of them, they were all different dogs but I named them all the same.

Sam Kelford
Blacksmith
Perth

I was a blacksmith pretty well all my life. In 1942 I came down here and rented a farm. But I was only on the farm a few days when they got me to come here and shoe horses. The old man took a heart attack and that was here, and I came here and shod horses and he died that fall with another heart attack or a stroke, I don't know which it was. So then I took the shop over in '44 and I've run it ever since. I hope I never have to retire from blacksmithing until I drop. I enjoy working for people, making things that they can't get, eh. I haven't shod a horse now for a long time. I work on machinery for the farmers now — parts that they can't get and parts that I can make it cheaper than they can buy it new. I make quite a few things that they can't get right away and that they need it tomorrow, eh, and they got to feed their cattle tomorrow and they got to feed them today and the thing breaks. Well, I make it up and let them get going. I was pretty small when I started working and I like to work yet. I never went to school, no education whatever. My boys have got to do my book work, what little bit of book work we do.

13

Flora Lazinskie
Polish Settler
Wilno

I'm Polish. You see, I was married in 1924 to a Blank. But "skie", I think that's Polish, eh. His name was Frank Blank. He was in the army in 1914. He was a veteran, and he was much older. I went to school till grade three. There was a teacher, and my goodness, was she ever cross, and I just got stubborn and said, "I'm just not going." Christmas was our jolly time. We had lots to eat. That's one thing we had. We killed so many pigs, so many cattle, but there was no such thing as deepfreezes and stuff like that, see. Sour cabbage was made in big barrels. Six, seven big barrels of pork. You see, it was salted and stuff like that. My mother used to make such good moonshine.

Percy Huckstep
Lime Kiln Labourer
Carleton Place

I had to quit working at the lime kiln on Napoleon St. I was married then and the wife told me to quit because I only got one eye and I would come home and the lime was burning the inside of my eyes and she thought maybe I would lose it in the other side, so she got me to quit. I lost my first eye in a car accident. I was fifteen years old. It was cut out and hanging down here on my cheek so they had to just nip it off and then I was blind in this eye for four days. I never had a car in my life. No, I never bothered, but I like going out for car drives. My brother, he had an old Ford to start off with. They used to go out on a Sunday for a drive and take their guns with them. And his old car had these running boards on them on the sides, you know, and he came to our place first before he went home and I remember one Sunday he came back and he had nine groundhogs on the runners. They'd take them home to skin them and eat them. The coin around my neck is the year I was born, 1911, June the fifth, 1911. I could of sold that one time up here at the midway. Last summer, one guy going there selling and buying different coins was bound that he was going to buy it. I said, "Nothing doing." I've had that for ages and I got that guy up in town, the jeweller, to drill a hole in it for me. It's not our money. It's a Newfoundland 50 cent piece.

Bill and Phyllis Miller
Trappers and Animal Lovers
Pakenham

I've been a trapper for 60 years and I have lived here all my life. I trap everything. You name it. Anything that flies up there or anything that walks on this earth. Yes, we have caught everything. We had all kinds of game here until they started to save the wolf, and take the bounty off the wolf. Our deer nearly went to nothing. The wolves were killing the deer right in our fields and the little fawns come wandering in here with the sheep. Little small fawns half starved, so starved they couldn't run away when you walked over to them. They just wobbled around. We had to pick them up and Phyll spent 300 dollars in canned milk to feed these little deer to keep them from starving. She brought them into the house sometimes here and, holy jeez, they were across the house so fast you couldn't get out of the road. We had three little deer in here for a little while, but they weren't here too long. We got them out to the barn and left them out there and they gradually walked away. They'd eat everything you're eating, eh? They like lettuce and they saw me putting mayonnaise on my lettuce so then they wouldn't eat lettuce unless it had mayonnaise.

Harold Gogo
Compulsive Trader
Kemptville

I've lived in this area for 25 years. I sell cars, trucks and tow. I sold 39 in the month of June; I sell on the average four or five a week. Now mind you, I don't make much money. I'll tell you they trade me anything. I should call it Gogo's Trading Post. Sometimes I get five or six new colour TV's, guns, anything they bring here and trade for the down payment and then I sell it. That's how I got that brand new TV. What do you think of that and no aerial!? Well, there is a coat hanger hanging out the window. That's how I got that one. I took that on a car deal. You name it — I got it, or did have it. It comes and goes. My great-grandfather was a horse trader and when I was going to school whatever I got at Christmas I'd take to school. Jackknives or wallets or anything; I would trade. Oh, I got the beautifullest jackknife years ago that you ever seen. And Mother said, "Don't you trade that jackknife, son." And I said, "Oh, no, Ma, I wouldn't trade that jackknife." I carried it for a week and then one day a guy said, "Here, what do you say we trade knives? I'll give you two for it." My mother said to my dad, "He's just going to be a real old trader just the same as your dad was." She said, "You'll starve to death when you grow up."

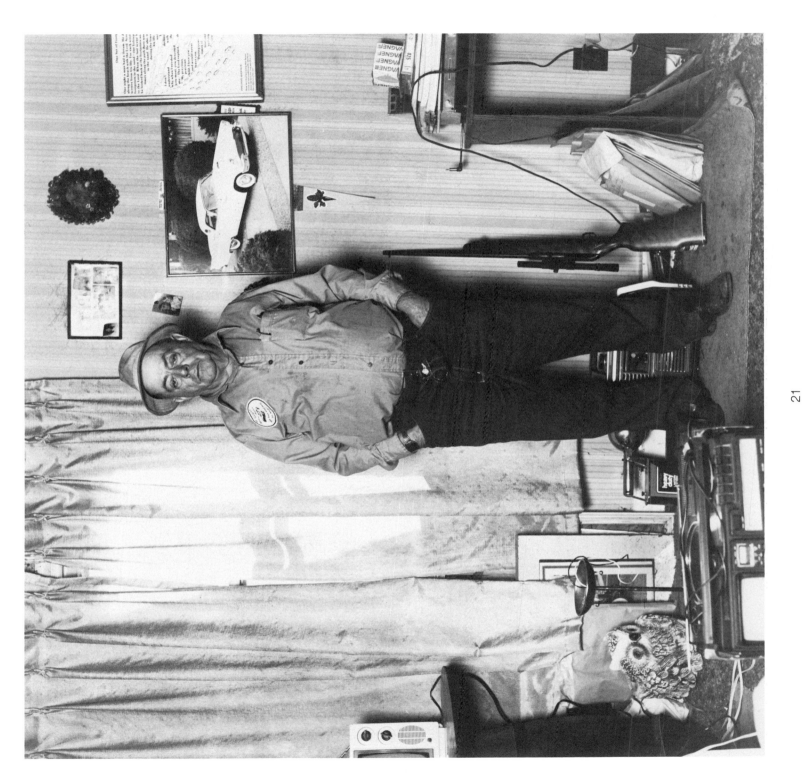

Leonard Best

Milkman
Renfrew

I don't know why I got into the milk business. I was working for my dad. He had bought a store up on main street there. Him and his brother and I was driving the bike, delivering for the grocery store and I guess I was getting ten dollars then and he said that he would give me 15 dollars a week. When I started milk was eight cents a quart now it's $1.20 and it's only a litre now, it's not a full quart. I automatically get up at four-thirty and I always eat before I go so I don't go till five-thirty. By six o'clock I'm on the road. When I first started we used to have horses. My horse's name was Brian. He knew where to stop and where to go and knew where people came out and fed him, give him apples or something. When you were in a place too long he'd turn and go to the next place, he'd only wait so long. He knew he was pretty smart. This is the only thing I would've done. I enjoy talking to the people, they miss me too. I had 172 customers in town, and in the morning I done it.

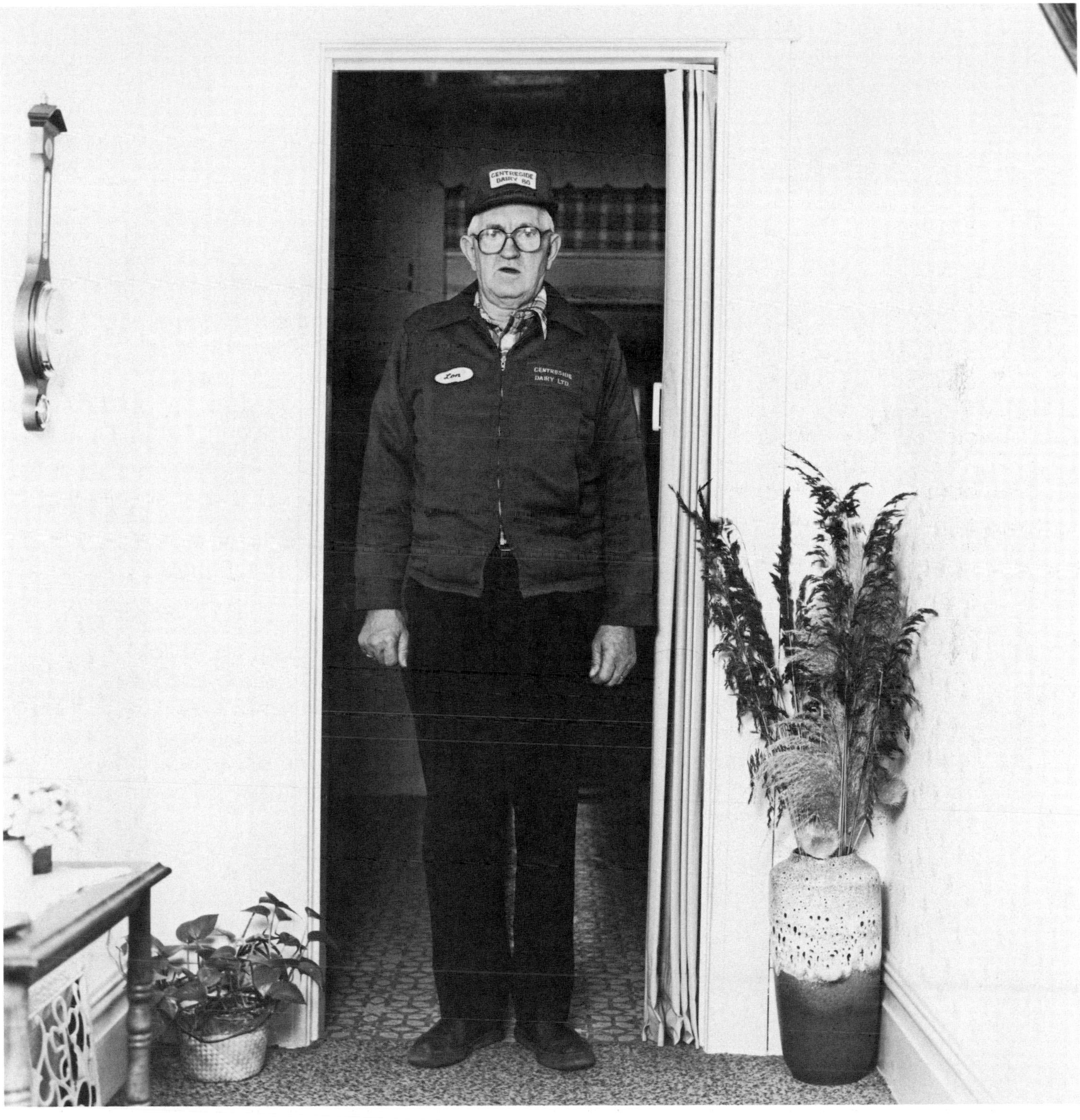
CENTRESIDE DAIRY 80
CENTRESIDE DAIRY LTD.

Michael Allen

Hearse and Ambulance Driver
Smiths Falls

I come here to look for a job. I was in Smiths Falls two and a half hours and I went to work at a Chinaman café waiting on tables. Well, I was there for three months and the Chinaman got me a job at the Imperial Oil service station up on the corner. From there I went to Mr. Amy. He was the undertaker. I drove an ambulance car for 28 years for the company. I worked for the funeral home too. I washed cars and polished cars and drove cars. All the car accidents and all that kind of stuff, I used to go with the ambulance car and I'd pick up the people that was in the cars. Well, it was a good job and if I didn't do it, somebody else was going to do it for me, so that was it. I either had to do it or quit, and there was too much money involved to quit. I enjoyed it because I know everybody in the bloody country. I enjoyed dressing up all the time and, of course, my bosses that I was involved with were the best that ever walked in a pair of shoes. If I'd done one thing, I'd stayed in school until I got a college education and I'd owned my own business by now. I'd owned a funeral business by now. I go downtown every day and there's a coffee club at the Woolworths. There used to be 15 of us but now there is only about eight or nine because all the guys is dead. But, Smiths Falls is a good little town, especially if you've got a job. If you got a job in this town it's all right.

Rene and William Bolger
Cattle Farmers
Clayton

I've lived here all my life, I was born right on the floor there with not even a bed to lie in. We have a 1,000 acre farm and we have beef cattle, we used to have dairy cattle. I was at the MacDonalds Corners fair and I won the first prize for the oldest man there, I got the cheque there the other day. I never won anything before in my life. I don't like travelling. I'd rather be in the bush cuttin' wood. There's too many people getting killed in airplanes. If I get killed in the bush I haven't got to fall out of the sky. They carry me in dead if they want to but they won't be carrying me out of the bottom of the ocean.

Allan Davidson
Historic Gun Owner
Opeongo Line

My grandfather settled here in 1880. He was the first man to have a horse up on the Opeongo here. And he went to Renfrew on horseback and they were looking for volunteers to go in the Riel Rebellion, you know out West, and he enlisted. And they walked from Renfrew to Brockville or Kingston, and they got into the boats there with the British army and they rowed them out, right up the Great Lakes. Rowed the whole way because there was no railroads at that time. He was gone two years and when he came back he brought the gun with him, and I still have the gun with a bayonet on it. That shot a lot of bear and deer after he brought it back. I used to shoot partridge with it. It was a muzzle loader. That's what I learned to shoot with. My mother's people were United Empire Loyalists. They come across from the States and settled down around Mallorytown. And they were millwrights. They used to go around making gristmills and sawmills. So they built a mill down here at Dacre and stayed there. They owned it. There was a lot of people who lived in this settlement at one time. It was all an Irish settlement. All that back up the Newfoundout, that's up the mountain there, they were all kinds of hillbillies you know. We own a thousand acres between me and my son. We raised ten kids, four orphan kids. We raised them because we just had one boy of our own and a daughter and the girl, to tell you the truth, had nobody to play with, so we thought we'd go and get her a girl to play with here, for company, and then that started and then they kept bringing them in. We had six or seven of them at one time. They were all nice kids.

Alex A. Schauer
Fiddle Maker
Cobden

I built a couple of guitars, you know, Hawaiian guitars, when I was 12 or 13. I think I charged four dollars for a guitar. I learned to play old-time music and I still play some. All my uncles on Dad's side were musically inclined. Dad played the fiddle and all my uncles played, and on my mother's side there was two boys played an accordian. The first fiddle I made from just local ordinary wood. I play on it sometimes. I'm also a collector. I have about 22 fiddles in the house. The first one I made out of an old maple dining room table that was imported from Germany back in the 1800's. For the neck I had to get a piece of wood, down near Haley's Station. It was a piece of five by five maple, a wooden thrashing mill. I got the neck part out of that and the top was made out of cedar and it came out of an old log building. If I knew all the tunes that I have learned from when I was 12 years old, I could play all night long from now until tomorrow morning at six o'clock and I wouldn't be playing the same tune twice.

Gordon Gurlitz Sr.

Quarry Worker
Eganville

I smoked at one time and I chewed tobacco at the same time, but I had to quit smoking for my job working in the quarry, handling dynamite. I'd be rolling a cigarette and loading a hole at the same time, especially these pop holes, you know. One day I just said, this is a little bit too dangerous. So I just threw the pack of tobaccy away. Of course, I still chewed tobacco.

33

Elwin Vaughan
Fire Chief
Richmond

The first fire truck cost 250 dollars. And we got it from the Ottawa fire department. It was an old ladder truck and they had scrapped it, you see, they had took it out of service, and we knew it was for sale. Joe and I went down to see it with Harold Moore, it's when he was Reeve. It was a great big long thing, you know, and I brought it up and shortened it up. I took one drive shaft out of it and cut eight feet off the back end of it. They had a great big wooden ladder on it and you couldn't turn it on the corner of the streets, you'd have to swing it way around the side and go around. I built a tank for it, 250 gallons and an air pump mounted on it with all the attachments. We used that for 10 years. Dr. Ryan took a heart attack. Well, the smoke was coming down the stairs about that high off the floor and I went on my hands and knees because the smoke was that thick. He had been sitting on the side of the bed and I guess he took a weak turn and he was smoking a cigarette and it fell between his legs and set fire to that. So I managed to get him up and I threw him across my shoulders and I headed for the door. He got to the hospital. Died next day. We broke the upstairs window and got the mattress out. You'd just get home here and get into bed and some of these old ladies would call up and ask, "Where's the fire?" I knew where everybody lived.

Cora Yuill
Poet
Almonte

I was born way up in Darling Township, way up above Clayton. I've lived in this house since 1947, and it was always a farm. The house, if you ask me, would be two hundred years old. It's an old, old house. I'm 81 years old, I feel pretty good. I love singing and I make up poem books, too. I gave away 70 this summer. I'd like to give you one. Would you take a poem book of mine? Thoughts on My Wedding Day was about my wedding day.

Thoughts on My Wedding Day

As I sit in my daughter's home,
my thoughts go back to a day.
On November 18, 1931,
when I heard those words obey.
It was a lovely day in November,
no snow lay on the ground.
Arthur drove the Model T Ford
and to Middleville we were bound.
Rev. McNabb was our minister
and at four o'clock that day,

we made our vows never to part
but things didn't stay that way.
On May 6 — year 1963,
when life seemed at its best,
Arthur was called from a world of care
to that home of peace and rest.
I'm all alone now, but my family of five
are just so good and kind.
I'll just enjoy each day as it comes
and leave the rest behind.

Jimmy and Myrtle Nesbitt
Well-Known Couple
Richmond

I was born in Twin Elm just below Richmond on July the fifth, 1905 and when I was two years old my parents bought a farm up on Queen Street beside the Roman Catholic Church and we lived there till 1917. The house was struck by lightning on the 14th of July and the buildings were struck with lightning on the second of September and burned, and so that fall my dad and mother were scared. The storms struck around there three or four times so they moved out of the village. Then, the fall of 1920, he bought here where we are now and we've been here ever since. I married Myrtle in 1940. We more or less stayed around here and travelled a bit. We started in 1971, I guess, to go to Florida and we've been going there every winter since. In fact we just got home two weeks ago. Right now I'm the oldest man in Richmond as far as the original ones from here.

Ferdinand Witt

Dairy Farming Through the Years

Pembroke

I started farming when I was, well, I never done anything else from the time I was out of school. I started farming on my own the year I got married. That was 1925, it was pretty much the same as it is now. We started farming with four cows. Well, the difference is now you're milking 40 or 45. When we got up in the morning the wife and myself and, once the boys got a little bit bigger, everybody got out to milk. Now there's two that go to the stable and they milk them 240 cows just as quick as we milked them four. You depended an awful lot on your neighbour. You worked together. You had no money to hire anything, you know, but one fellow helped the other fellow. You weren't in such a rush. If you got to the line fence with the plow and the neighbour was coming up, you kind of held back a little bit so you could get there too and then you would have a little chat for about 15 or 20 minutes. But today you're darn lucky if you can say how do you do to him when you're passing him, because nobody has any time for nothing. It's just go. We used to get up around five o'clock and we'd go and milk and then we would have our breakfast. But if you were pulling out with the horses after seven o'clock you kind of snuck out in case the neighbour would see you, you were kind of ashamed of yourself of being after seven. That's the time when you want to get out in the fields. Get up early in the morning and you don't have to work after dark. My dad always claimed that if you can't make a living in ten hours there's something wrong with your management.

41

Stan Morton
Variety Store Owner
Almonte

I was born in Almonte in 1910, and then, in 1924, I went to work in a woollen company as a bobbin boy. That's one of the first jobs they had for kids. I worked there altogether 27½ years. In 1952, my wife was a cashier in a grocery store and the grocer met me on the street one day and asked me if I'd like to go and help him in the store. And I said, "Well Harry, I don't know anything about groceries and I wouldn't know corn flakes from beans or whatever." "Oh," he said, "well, you'll learn." I worked 15 years for him. Shortly after that, this store came available and my wife and I decided that we would throw everything we could scratch up into a fund and buy this thing from the lady that wanted to sell it. And we did that and started on the first of January. Lets see, this is my 20th year. We have long hours here in the store. I come over in the morning before eight o'clock and we close at six. My wife died eight years ago and I decided to carry on. My wife's sister works for me and I have another lady who was with the store when I bought it and she stayed on. So we're all senior citizens, actually. The time will come to sell when I think I can't handle it any more. So far that doesn't seem to be the case, I'm still happy. It's a real good hobby, it's an incentive to get up in the morning.

43

Tom Jessup
Centenarian
Eganville

I'm 103, so they say. They say hard work can kill you but I don't believe it. I farmed all my life. It's about five or six years ago I quit. I was born in Brudenell township, oh way back. The young lads now, I tell ya, they have all kinds of play toys and everything to play with but us young lads, we'd go out and turn over a stone and start playing with the crickets and the ants under the stones. That's all we had to play with. Walk, walk, walk. I've seen me walking when I come in after my breakfast. I'd walk for a couple of hours looking for sheep in the bush. Come in, throw myself on the couch and lay there till I got rested. Go and throw the harness on the horses and follow them in the field. Then it's time to hunt the cows again, go again two or three miles. Played out. It was hard. They know nothing about it now. Go to work and jump on some machinery and away they go. Sit down and do it. So if hard work kills you, I think I would've been dead a long time ago. More people dies from laziness than hard work.

Harry Seabrook
Lifetime of Farming
North Gower

I was born in North Gower and I spent 75 years on that farm. I was born on the farm, raised on the farm and, until I retired, I lived on the farm. It was a dairy farm. My whole life is farm, that's all I know. The farmers never suffered from the rationing because we always had our own food. We'd make seven crocks of butter in the fall of the year and that would do us till the cows were on grass the next spring.

J.A. Sabourin
Police Interpreter
Cumberland

I worked with the police as interpreter. I remember the last hanging in L'Orignal. This was 53 years ago. It was always the hangman that made the scaffold because he had the blueprints. We needed a piece of wood with no knots, pine 18 inches thick I think, but no knots. So we went in the yard, the sheriff and I. We chose the piece of wood but when it was planed we could see knots; before you couldn't see them. So we ordered another one. The owner knew the sheriff and I and he asked, "What in the hell are you going to do with this?" He told us after, when we went to pay, he says, "If I had have known it was to hang anyone, I wouldn't have sold it to you." The night of the execution, it was after twelve o'clock, and they followed me up the scaffold. I had a big ladder and lights and it was raining and slippery. They always asked him if he has anything to say before he dies, so he didn't have anything to say. So the trap it opens, just like this, and the doctor goes up to see if he is dead and he decided that he was dead and then the hangman takes his knife and cuts the rope and then they put him in a box, not a coffin, an ordinary box built with ordinary lumber. And then we went to get the other one and that was the hardest that time, the second one. If there had've been a third one I couldn't of stand it either. My daughter was born the same evening of the execution.

Bill Leckie
Carpenter
Burnstown

I'm interested in wood and interested in things that I make, you understand. I do the best I can for anybody and everybody, as far as I'm able and that's all I can do. It keeps your mind busy and if you keep your mind busy you're an awful lot healthier and better if you were old. I've been living here all my life and that's over 83 years. I can remember when we cut pine logs here and we got one bunch of it sawed into 12 inches, all 12 inches wide and 12 feet long. We piled that out and dried it and drew it to Renfrew and got $22.00 a 1,000 for it. Now what the hell would you get for it now? Now when I built this place 30 years ago that kind of lumber, 12 inch lumber, was worth about a dollar a foot, and now what is it? And not the good quality either. When I built this house I ripped a lot of 12 inch boards for clapboards, you know, to make them narrow before I got them dressed. I built a little saw for myself and a saw table out of oak. And I ripped all that stuff to cover the house. All done myself and I didn't have anybody helping me, and I built this myself. I drew out a plan on a piece of paper and I put in where I wanted the windows and doors. I thought I was going to be stuck one time but I didn't. I got out of it. I hate like hell to be beat.

Sarah Lavalley
Dedicated Worker
Golden Lake Reserve

I met the Pope. I went over to Rome, yes, I met him in Rome. That picture was taken in the big church. We had a big audience in the church, and those who got a front seat got to shake hands with him. I got the Pope's Medal for the highest honour a woman could get in the Catholic religion. I worked for the Church since I was married. In fact, I was keeping house for the priest when I got married in Eganville. That's another award for the highest honour, the Canada Medal. You've heard of the Canada Medal for good citizenship. I don't know why I got all these medals; I didn't work to get anything. I did work all right; I did a lot of work. The work had to be done and there was nobody else to do it so I just kept on doing it. I work for the reserve a lot, I did a lot of work on the reserve. Things weren't going the way they are now, you know, years ago. It was hardship on the reserve, there was a lot of people hardup. There was one good thing I got on the reserve and they're still making out on it and that's making snowshoes. I was born on the reserve and I am 91 years old. I'll be 92 next April. Well, I never think of my age anymore. I try and forget about it. When you get that old you can't plan very much any longer; you just plan for today, not for tomorrow or next week because you don't know if you're going to be there or not. My husband just died two years in January, he was 92 when he died.

Silas and Henrietta Boyd

Busy Farmers
Carp

I've been married 50 years to the same woman. Fifty years married and 81 years young. I haven't used a chainsaw this winter because it's been bad weather. The bush was that wet. You couldn't get in the first part. Then the snow come. I just knocked around, lazy. I started farming here in 1925. We moved out here on the 14th of April and started to plow. I haven't farmed for some time now. The day we got married was good but the night turned out to be awful. Rough, stormy night. We had a platform out on the lawn at the homestead and all, but there was thunder and lightning all night. There was maybe 30 or 40 people at it. We had a good time. And then, on our 50th anniversary we had a big day. Oh, there was people there I hadn't seen for a long time. The 50 years go quick — too quick. It's crazy. I've had a busy life. I've always kept going, always kept going. It didn't do me any harm. Somebody that would sit around and lay around most of their life they're gone long ago. Hard working never killed you if you don't get hurt.

Joe Crawford and Harold Majaury

Bachelor Cousins
Hopetown

It's been three years since I came here to live with Harold. He lived across here in a white house. He was over there for eight years. I never got married, I was too wise for that. The two of us live here, both bachelors. We're second cousins. My grandmother and his father are brother and sister. I was born in Darling, it was quite a while ago. I'm not young, I'm ninety-one. I worked in the lumber camps pretty well all the time, all up through that north country. You'd go in in the fall and come out in the spring. It was a good life. I'd do it again if I had good legs. I like the work in the bush. We used to log up around Flower Station and Clyde Forks, T.A. Wilson Lumber Co. I never went to school. His mother died when he was young. He was put out to a home. I don't know how they got away without sending him to school. He was kept home to do chores. It was hard times living in the Depression. He cooks his own food and I do the same.

57

Albert Griffin
Cabinetmaker
Almonte

I learned to be a cabinetmaker by doing what I was told. I wanted to be one. I wouldn't of been anything else, it was in the family, you see. My father died when I was quite young; I don't even remember him and he was a cabinetmaker and an undertaker and a wheelwright. I was born in Lestershire, England. I came over here in 1947 because you don't learn anything if you don't travel a little bit. If I didn't have liked it over here I wouldn't have stayed; I'd have gone somewhere else. I've been a cabinetmaker ever since I was 16; I learned it by using hand tools. There was no machines when I was a kid. We use machines now because it's quicker. Don't say it's better. It's quicker. I'm going to turn 80 next year. I just got a letter from my brother's son this morning. He passed away. That's my next older brother. I'm the last of the family now. Everybody has to kick the pail somehow or other sometime. You can't do anything about it. We were never very close, Lawrence and I, never close at all. I don't know if he was different. No, correction — I was different. My mother always said that I was different. Something different about you. She said I was queer, but not queer queer, I was funny queer. I like science fiction books, but it's hard to get hold of a good one now. I've been reading science fiction ever since I was ten or twelve years old. My stepfather said you'd drive yourself crazy with that. It's like I told him — I can never forget, he used to say, "Oh, you'll drive yourself crazy." He had a magazine for boys and there was articles on sports which I was never interested in. I couldn't kick a ball. I couldn't throw one. I couldn't catch one. I couldn't hit one with a baseball bat or a cricket ball. Oh, Lord, I couldn't be bothered.

Edgar Getz
General Store Owner
Killaloe Station

We come from Rockingham. I started the store up here and I was at it for 33 years. I quit about three years ago; I took a bad heart attack, and only for that I'd still be at it. I miss the public, you know, having a chat with people. There was all kinds of them came there in the summertime, and I knew everybody so you miss those things, you know. And I worked up a very good business, a very good business. I started with nothing. I knew the traveller that was travelling for a wholesale outfit in Renfrew. And I asked him, "Would you give me credit?" and I said, "I need lots of it." So he went on holidays and he didn't tell me I owed them $2,500 and that was a hell of a pile of money in those days, you see. And the boss came in, the fellow who owned the outfit. He said, "Have you got an order today, Mr. Getz?" and I said, "Yes." And so I gave him the order and he said, "Thank you very much." And away he went. And I thought, who the hang is that fellow anyways? So when the regular came back again I said, "Who was here last week?" "Oh," he said, "That's the owner of the outfit." I darned near dropped to the floor. He never asked me for the money or anything, and I paid them. It took some time, you know, and I paid them. You see, if you run a general store, you got to work, you open early in the morning and you're open seven days a week and you want to stay open till ten every night, and you're going to make it go. But if you don't do that, you wouldn't survive, you see.

Harry Hinchley
Town Historian
Renfrew

I started writing for the Renfrew Mercury some years ago after I retired. I was an office man before I retired. I worked in Renfrew and other places too. So I retired and I got something to do. I've always been interested in history, more or less. Some people couldn't care less. People running a newspaper aren't wrong to put in old material because the old people like to see that. This house is approaching 100 years I guess, I don't know. No one seems to know. There's a lovely old house up on the corner. It's too bad they have to put all those modern houses up. They should leave the old ones there; the old houses have their own character. They had the finest old mansion up there at the end of the street and they demolished it. There were a lot of fine old schools too, but a lot of them were torn down and made into a house or something.

Sally Coward
Music Composer
Carleton Place

When I first started, I didn't know anything about composing. I used to make one hand go with the other and I worked at that all by myself till I was about six. I went to Halifax during the war. I played for a lot of places. I'd go to eat, I'd play the piano for the different restaurants and the Salvation Army for the boys during the war. A lad that I liked wrote poetry. Well, you can't neck all night. So we used to take his poetry and I'd try and put it to music. So I wrote a song called, well he had entitled it "Echo of a Song". Oscar Peterson was playing at the Alberta Lounge, just before he went to Carnegie Hall, and I went up to the piano and I said, "I wonder if you would hear a song of mine" and he said, "Of course." So he went down to the audience and I played up on the grand piano, and he came up to the piano after I got through, played it right through. He never even watched my fingers, he put all the notes down sitting in the audience and that, to me, is miraculous. So he came up and he played the piece and he called me and he said he's going to play it over CJAD in Montreal on a certain night. And I was just thrilled to pieces to hear it.

John Joe O'Brien

Bushman
Eganville

We lived here 25 years about. I came from up the Opeongo, they call it Esmond. It's just up above Joe Dellaire. We'll be 25 years married on the 17th of July. I was in the bush and farmed all my life, there was not much work them years, when I was young, only farming. I poke around a little on the sticks, I got a pretty bad foot and leg.

Grant Christie
Reeve and Store Owner
Heckston

I'm the reeve of South Gower Township. I became reeve in 1965 I guess, and I was 12 years on the council before that. I've never been out. Thirty-four continuous years this fall. I don't think I'll go in again. One more year is election year. You got to call it quits sometime. I've had the store here since 1975, and before that I farmed. I'd rather run the store because I'm not in shape to farm now, I couldn't stand it. We open at eight in the morning and close at nine at night or nine-thirty or just whenever they leave. There's a lot of people in and out and a lot of visits — a lot of lies told. We had a fellow in here with a shirt over his head one night and tried to take the money box here but we caught him. That type of thing doesn't make you nervous, it makes you hellish mad. You're damn right, if I had a crowbar or something that night, he would never have got out of here because I would've floored him. It would've been possible. There was a fire here in '79 — February of '79. We lost everything. We lost all the stock and everything, and the only thing that was left was the floor. We managed to salvage that and cover it again. Oh yes, the whole darn thing went. We have no idea what started it. It burned down right at noon hour. I had one customer in here. It used to be divided into two parts. Back in here we used to keep our stock and stuff and I just opened the door to get in there and the flames just hit me. She went and she went in a hurry, oh gawd. It wasn't three minutes till the windows blew out.

69

Frank Marquette
World War I Vet
Smiths Falls

I was born in Smiths Falls 89 years ago last December. I fought in World War One. In 1918 I was wounded in the leg. I got a shrapnel ball there that they took out of my leg. I remember getting hit. It was a big shell you see and they're full of junk and everything. I was in France and I was in the hospital six weeks and then I went back to the battalion after that. I didn't come home because the war wasn't over. My leg was bandaged with bandages even when I was back on the line. They had me back in there. We slept in the mud and had a snooze. We had cans of bully beef. We called it bully beef but it was corned beef. When I came back to Smiths Falls I came back to the railroad, I was assistant yardmaster for a while and yard foreman. There was about 1,800 railroad people here at one time and then the running trade like trainman and conductors and engineers and fireman. There were almost a 1,000 men who had to report for watch inspection. They had to have their pocket watches inspected all the time. My father before me was on the railroad.

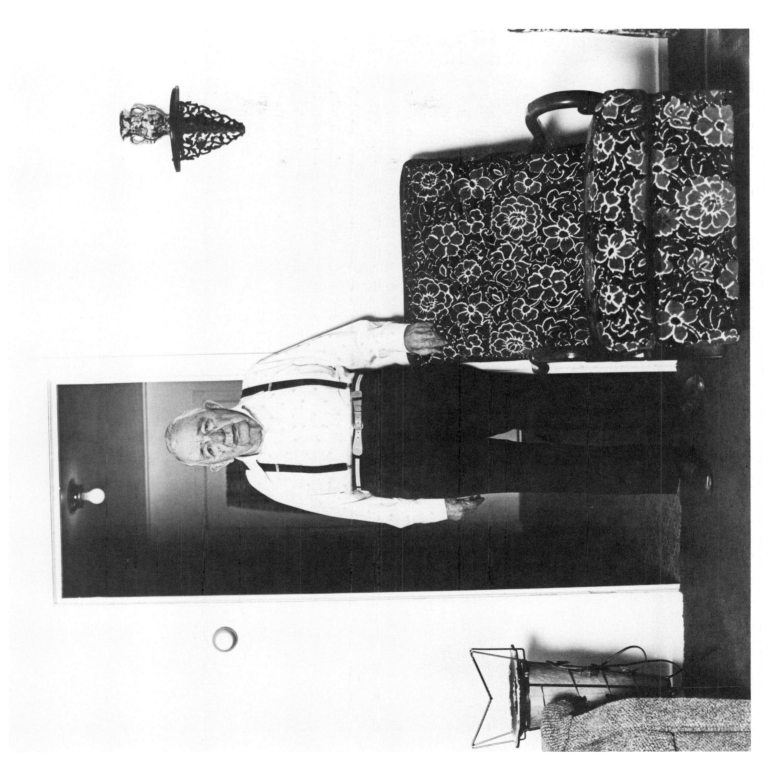

Ivan Hart
Country and Western Fan
Poland

I was born in Poland back in a old place. I've been here since 1970 in this house here. My dad and mother and I, we sold the old farm back over there. It's ten years today that my dad died and my mom's been in the Lanark Lodge. Not too many people live in Poland, you can see it all driving through. It's not a Polish community. There used to be a place over the hill there called the Warsaw Hotel. It's mostly Scottish that settled here. I never got married. I never had a car of my own to go out and chase women, and now I'm not able. This used to be the old school. I went to school here, I quit school here in 1939. I slammed the door never thinking that 30 or 40 years later I'd end up living in the place. There's a picture of MASH up there on the wall. I loved that show. I use to watch it when it was on. It's not on now, is it? And I used to love the Dukes of Hazard, I'm trying to get a picture of them especially that Daisy Duke. I doubt that I can get one. And that one of Dolly Parton came in an album one time. I like country and western music. The radio goes from when I get up in the morning till I go to bed or decide to watch television. The only rock and roll I ever listened to is that show on television. It's off too now these last two years, Solid Gold with the women dancing in it. I like that. There's not much to watch Sunday night so I listen to the radio, CKBY. I never miss Ralph Carlson's show. I had a few drinks with Ralph. Oh yes, he's been in the Revere Tavern. He'd come and sit with us and he bought us a drink and we bought him a drink. He mentioned my name on the radio one Sunday night. He said, "For a friend of mine." He played "Carolina in the Pines". That's not my favorite song. It's one by Ricky Scaggs but its OK, he mentioned my name.

Emerson Kohlsmith

Early Education

Cobden

I was born in Cobden 62 years ago. I went to the Number One Ross schoolhouse which was built in 1865, a one room school. I didn't start to school till I was nine because I had polio when I was four years of age. I went to grade 12. I went longer than any of my brothers on account of me being with a bum leg, and I tried to get a little education.

Bill Wylie
Horseman
Carleton Place

I was overseas in England in '40 and that's where I lost this. I was with the Stormont, Dundas and Glengarry Highlanders. I got married over there on the 18th of November 1944. Still married and still the same woman. I show standardbred horses and I had some saddle breds when the kids were small. I had a saddle bred mare and I had some kid's ponies too and we used to have a big pony club here. We had 45 kids here for about three years. I have one horse in the barn here and I have a stallion in Ottawa. I had 23 horses here at one time. In 1971 I won the speed and show class both at the Royal Winter Fair. I have 270 some ribbons there and there's a bunch downstairs in a box and I've given a lot to my sons — they've wanted them. I put them out and keep the birds out of the berries — they blow. Yes we've always been horse crazy, I guess, us fellows. I'll be at a Fair and my sisters will be there and they'd be saying we never saw you. Well, I'll tell you one thing I wasn't playing bingo. If you want to see me you got to come where the horses is.

Wilbert and Florence Munro

Square Dancers
Clayton

I was born in this house 77 years ago. My grandfather bought this farm for 89 cents an acre, 200 acres. My wife came from up around at Dacre. I'd called in at my brother's place not knowing that she was there, eh, but she happened to be there, you see, and they made me acquainted with her. I said, "What are you going to do Saturday evening?" And she said, "Nothing." Well, I said, "I'll be down to pick you up." And that was the start of it. We went together for about a year. I had an old Model T Ford, you see, and I'd go way up through this back road by Calabogie, it's 50 miles up by that way. I could go up on two gallons of gas and come back on a gallon and a half because there was more downhill coming home. And the gas was 25 cents a gallon and I could make it for 85 cents. We were married 53 years on the fourth of October. I was ten years on the school board, you see, 13 years on council. I love running these elections. We had a second election one year at White Lake. They weren't pleased. They thought some of the women should have got a vote, you see, so they called a second election. I like the square dancing music, we square dance all over the country. We belong to the Old Time Fiddlers in Perth and the Old Time Fiddlers in Lanark and we dance all over. If I had a dollar for every square I'd take a trip around the world. But today there's not too many that know how to do it, you know, the right way. I've danced 12 squares in a night. A square is five changes you see.

Elizabeth Hunt
Cottage Keeper
Constan Lake

I was born at Black Donald, the place that we are living on right now is my mother's oldest sister's home. I'm here 23 years. I had eight children and I was 85 on Easter Sunday. I liked Black Donald. I wouldn't trade it for all the places around here put together. We had a beautiful lake but now they flooded it and I won't go back there. I don't want to see it. They flooded it because they built a big dam, a big power dam. Ontario Hydro flooded us out and they gave us a damn dirty deal. The Hydro is one of the meanest, rottenest. What they gave me wouldn't buy one little cottage on this lake today and I had over seven acres right on the front and I had lots of cottages. They're a rotten bunch to deal with and I would say it. I started collecting salt and pepper shakers in 1942. I have in the thousands, I don't know, I can't tell you, I quit counting them because you start to wash them and put them back up and the phone rings and I get mixed up in my counting. I like them though.

Walter Cameron
Blacksmith and Philosopher
Fallbrook

A blacksmith was a very important man in every community. I've had a good life and a useful life. Enjoyed the whole thing. Four generations of our family has worked on that anvil. That's history. This old shop was built in 1865, that's 121 years ago, isn't it? I never liked going to school. I went to public school up here and I didn't like it and Mother got me persuaded to go to high school for one year, the longest year I ever put in in my life. I came home and my father was hammering away. He was a good blacksmith, and I poked around for awhile. He's a man that didn't do any foolin', you know, Highland Scotsman. I said to him, "I think I'll learn the trade with you," and he stopped, put one hand on each end of the anvil, stood there for what I thought was a long time. After awhile he said, "Well Walter, if that's what you're thinking about you have two choices. You can either learn to be the best tradesman you can be, or on the other hand, you can learn how to make excuses." Twenty-five years from that very day I was second vice president of the Master of Horses in Ontario. See what my father did. I shod a purebred Morgan mare on my 90th birthday a year ago last fall. It's a world record. There was 1,000 people here that day — big event. They were here from all over. I tell everybody I don't know nothing, then you can get away with asking questions. People tell me I've got some philosophy. I get along all right I just know nothing. I'm not young enough to know it all.

Vernon Price

Lumberjack
Beachburg

The best memory I have of a lumber camp was when I walked seventeen miles into that camp there. I knew the foreman, and I said, "I want a job." "Well gawd", he said, "we're turning men away every day," but he said, "Come on in and stay the night." So in the morning the foreman always calls the men. He opens the door and shouts aboard. Well everybody left but me so he says would you go on the main road. I says, "I'll go anywhere." So I went on the main road; that's the worst job, the worst job in the world. But anyway I was very fortunate and about nine o'clock he came along and he said, "Look it, Price," he said, "Do you want a team and go and skid?" Well sir, even to this day I've never heard as nice a music in my life. But if I give you a cadillac car and a swindle sheet to go with it, you wouldn't appreciate it near as much as I did to get the job.

I was a shanty man for two years. The first time I ever ate a hamburg was in a lumber camp. The tremendous work that the cook had to do. He had to cut it all up and he had to cull all the meat off the bone and put it through a hand grinder, eh. He had to chop it up for 100 men and they made it about that thick and all loaded with onions. Well, nobody ever tasted hamburg in those days. Like any meat that we cut off got made into a stew. I don't know how many I ate, but I knew I should quit because he had raisin pie there that thick, just melt in your mouth, and I knew I should quit because I wanted two pieces of pie. It was a hell of a position to be in, eh?

George Budd
German Farmer
Eganville

I've smoked since I was young, some 23 years ago, just tobacco and rolling papers. I also smoked pine needles and clover. I got sick from my first cigarette. Even chewing tobacco got sick on it. We're German but I never want to go to Germany and see where our parents came from because you'll never get me up in a plane. I went up once and that's enough. I went up in a single motor passenger plane, and that's enough by jeez boy. Too gawd damn many hijackers and stuff going on. You never know once you're up there, if he pulls a gawd damn gun on you, well, you could come down or you could fall down. We own 200 acres here and it's half bush. You have your own wood and stuff like that. We use a wood stove. We're going to sell that one, and we're going to buy a smaller one. Do you know anybody that wants to buy an electric stove? Thirty, 35 dollars for it, and at least 300 dollars for the wood stove. That's a heavy old bastard, boy.

Mary MacDonald
Big Family
Tatlock

I had 20 births and I have two pair of twins. I was 17 when I had my first one and I was 44 when I had my last one. They all say, "How did you manage?" but of course, one kind of looked after the other, I guess and I never had much trouble with them. These days people don't have big families because they can't afford it. It's different when they're going to school now. Ours mostly went to this little school down here a mile away and they weren't particular about the clothes they wore. You didn't have to be dressed right up, you know the way they do now. Most of the kids were born at home. They were all born at home but three. We used to have beef and pork and every morning you'd have rolled oats porridge. For Christmas the girls would get a doll if we could afford it at all. They wouldn't get very much, they always got some little thing. Kids have too much now.

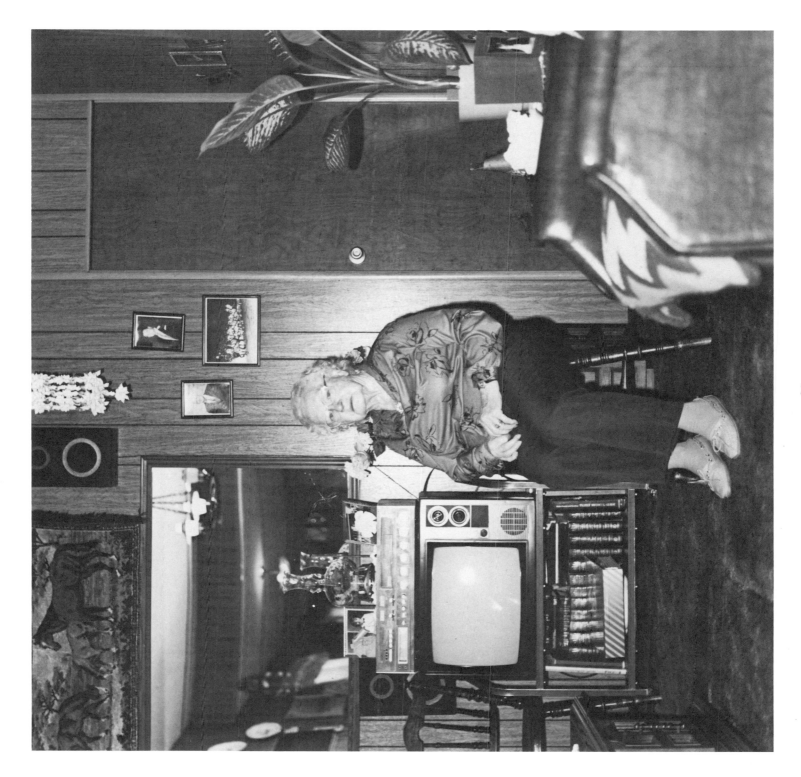

Gordon Caldwell
Country Butcher
Lanark

I haven't retired yet and I don't think I ever will, there's too much fun here. Right now we're cutting up a moose, I don't know whether you can smell it but I can. One deer hunting season, one week or two weeks, or whatever it is, I had 39 deer hanging in here, not skinned. We're going to have to put a stop to that though, they're going to have to skin them before they can bring them in. I like butchering, but I can't kill, let the slaughterhouse do that. We used to kill out at people's places, and I had a butcher working for me, and he done the sticking of them. The law got tougher on them and now we have a slaughterhouse, and when there's any killing done the Inspector is called and he is standing right there. I turned down a bear the other day, I'm not going to put them into my kill room because they smell like anything. I started the lockers. Before the home freezers started, lockers had sprung up here and there over Ontario. So I got a carpenter and we insulated this big room and then you bought the locker boxes. Then I put in a little meat counter and it gradually grew from there, and I started to custom-cut. You roll up your sleeves and you go at it.

90

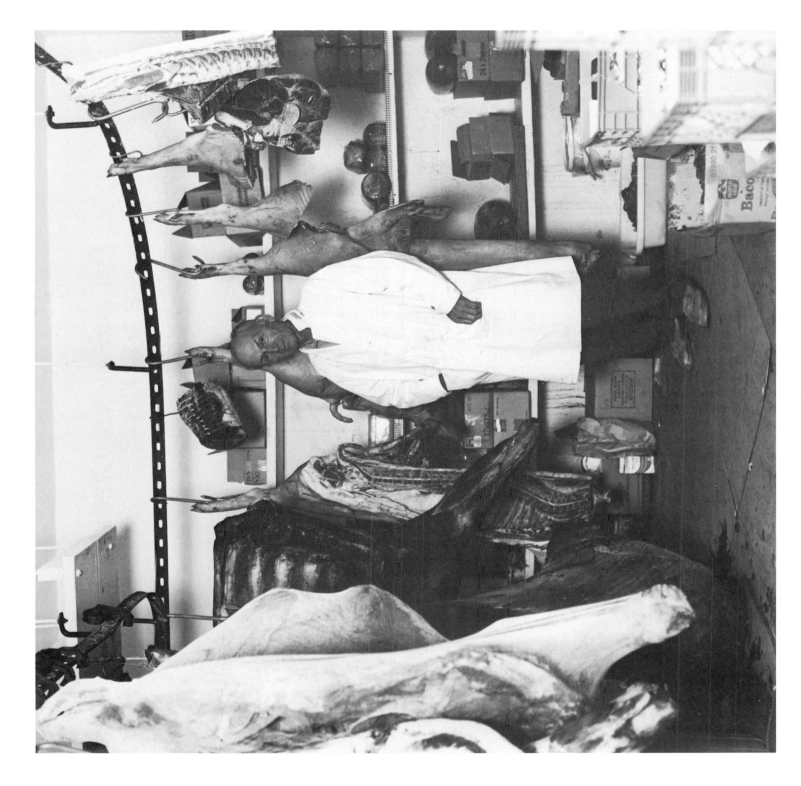

Del and Angela Green
Railroad Worker
Richmond

The CNR stockyard was opened in Richmond about 1913. One day the gate was inadvertently left open and a large hog strayed onto the track and was killed by train number 39. The following was written by the late Roy Laffin, requesting recompense from the CNR for the loss of his hog.

My razor-back strayed on the track, a week ago today,
Old 39 came up behind and sniffed his life away.
You can't blame me, this hog, you see,
Strayed through the stockyard gate,
So kindly pen your cheque for ten
This bill to liquidate.

A week later the reply from the CNR came.
Your hog was killed upon our tracks,
This we most truly know.
But razor-backs on railroad tracks
Must surely come to woe.
The cheque for ten which you pen,
We sadly must decline,
Go bury the dead, write o'er his head
Here lies a foolish swine.

Joe Hogan
Longtime Reeve
Cormac

I was reeve for 13 years. I've been connected some way with council, I suppose, all my life that I was here. My father was on council. There was no money in it. You got, I suppose at the start, 15 or 20 dollars a meeting and that sort of thing and by the time I left you got 35 dollars a meeting which was once a month. You couldn't live off it. The township give me a silver tray at a retirement banquet in February of last year. I made up this lament. I forget just what the lament was and I just turned it into this:

I've been balled out and balled up, bulldozed, blackjacked, walked on, cheated, squeezed and mooched. Stuck for war tax, excess profits tax, state tax, dog tax and sin tax, liberty bond, baby bond, and the bond of matrimony. I've been asked to help the Society of St. John the Baptist, J.A.R., women's relief, and stomach relief. I have worked like the devil and have been worked like hell. I have been drunk and got others drunk, and last of all I had to part with my furniture, and because I won't spend or lend all of it till I go beg, borrow or steal, I've been cussed and discussed, boycotted, talked to and talked about, lied to and lied about, robbed and darn near ruined and the only reason I'm sticking around now is to see what hell is coming next.

Dora Rousselle

Sweepstakes Winner

Arnprior

I won the Irish sweepstakes in 1969. I got a rabbit's foot. I guess that's what brought me good luck, but it wasn't such good luck for the rabbit that got killed. My husband had died, and lots of times I got darn phone calls that you didn't like sometimes or just to scare you and that day, on the 20th of March, I heard the phone ringing and I thought it was somebody else kidding me, you know. He said, "Mrs. Rousselle, we have a telegram for you from Ireland," and I said, "Have you got any more of those jokes? You can keep them to yourself." And I hung up. And so he phoned back again and he said, "I'll deliver it myself." So he did. I'm still on the tail end of it. The first thing I did after? Well first of all, I said, "Give me a tranquilizer before I pass out.

Vic Thompson
War Vet
North Gower

I got to be a major but I came through the ranks. I started out as a private soldier. I was in the artillery the whole time. In World War II I was in Britain for quite awhile and I got into action on the second front and I crossed over into France on the push to go in on D Day but they had an administration foul up as usual. Those of us that were supposed to go in as spares for observing officers were reported lost so they flew people over to replace us and in the meantime the fellow that replaced me was killed, so I never argued. I was talking to a fellow one time and the Germans started to shell us and I turned around to say another word to him and there he was with his head off. I was just in the middle of a conversation and we weren't as far apart as you and I. I was out for some years and then I went back in for Korea, and I was there for 13 months. I came back then I decided that I might as well stay in and get to be pensionable so I stayed on for years. I put in about 26 years in the military or something like that. I got a letter from the Korean government about ten years ago thanking me very much for my service in saving their country and they said, "Would you be prepared to come and help us again if it become necessary?" So I wrote back and said, "You just kind of forgotten what my age is." I said, "Thanks very much for the compliment."

William John Walther
The Farming Life
Foymount

I was born here 86 years ago in June, I was born here and I'm here yet. I farmed all my life, it was dairy. Years ago you had to make a living a little different than now. You had to produce everything. You kept pigs, you kept hens, you kept cows, and you'd milk the cows and make the butter. My dad wasn't well and when I was 12 or 13 I started to plow. I never had a tractor here. I did all my work with horses until I quit. I done a lot of walking. I done all my plowing and harrowing. Legs have given up now but I don't wonder. There's a lot more vacant farms now. There were all mostly fairly big families, you know, and you'd go back and forth. Oh, I remember some good times. You had house dances. You'd walk. You'd think nothing of walking eight or ten miles to a dance. We used to have box socials at the school. The girls would bring a box and they'd auction them off and make money for the school and the boys would buy the boxes and if you knew your girl's box then you could buy it and if you didn't you'd buy someone else's. They'd have a nice lunch in it; sandwiches and cake and sometimes, if you were a smoker, a box of cigarettes. Then they'd have a dance. They had a violin, maybe two violins, if they could get them.

Lawrence Pelton

Cheesemaker
Hyndman

My uncle started the cheese business in 1898. I took it over in the early 1930s. The name never changed until this past year. A firm in Vancouver wanted the name worse than we did so we eventually gave it to them. We had a chap come in with us in 1953, I think it was, and he brought the name in as Dairy Land Foods. Now it's called Hyndman Foods. I've been too ill the past little while and I haven't worked too much. We sell some cheese in town and some around the area stores and neighbouring district. We go through about 20,000 litres of milk a day. In the old days there were some that made their own cheese, but not too many. There were quite a number of factories around the area. In Eastern Ontario we had about 150 factories, small factories and some of them not so small either. They were a very good size. There's only three factories left now in Eastern Ontario. A lot of them were bought out. Big money came along. I guess I was too bullheaded to get bought out. I would've made more money if I had of been bought out but my business would of been gone. We sell about a million pounds of cheese a year, I guess.

Alvie and Margaret Strong

Newlyweds
Renfrew

We were married in April of this year. I met him after coffee hour, that's where I first saw him. They always have a little tea party for new members. Somebody asked me, "Do you see that man over there?" and I said, "Yes, and I can't keep my eyes off him either." I said, "The one with the white hair" and she said, "Do you know who he is?" and I said, "Alvie Strong." We stood and talked for a little while and he almost missed his lunch that day. We were engaged from December till April. I got my ring in December, the 17th of December. Our wedding was a big occasion here and I really think they went all out. The Presbyterian minister came and married us here in the Bonnechere Manor auditorium. The place was packed. We were just going to get married and go to the restaurant but when they found out about it they put up a reception and a luncheon. There was no liquor and no confetti.

Gladys Dowdall
Congenial Newspaper Worker
Carleton Place

I was born in England and I was two when I came to Canada. We came to Carleton Place and here we stayed. I never wanted to live anywhere else. I love the people. My daughter used to say she hated to go downtown with me because I stopped for an hour at every corner to talk. I love the Valley all the way through because all the people are so nice, they're so friendly. My poor mother, she near died from loneliness and couldn't stand the cold winters but we loved it. I can remember when I came to this town, my gawd there was only dirt roads and wooden sidewalks — the horse and buggy days. This is where we saw our first cow. My brother, that was two years older than me, he was fascinated. People right next door to us had two cows, two Jerseys. I'll always remember that. We'd go over there and get a pail of milk. We were so fascinated with that silly old cow. I went to work at the Carleton Place Canadian. I was more or less hired as just a receptionist, answer the telephone and look after the people at the counter and I thought that wasn't enough to do. Little by little I picked up this and picked up that, run the old address-o-graph machine and addressed all the papers by just cranking the machine. And there was thousands of them to do. It's nice when you start from the bottom, you know. But I enjoyed it because I couldn't have sat on my rear end at a desk all day pounding a typewriter. To me that's the dullest job in the world. I met all kinds, and loved the people. And at Christmas time you always got a box of chocolates from this one and a bottle of wine from that one and a box of cookies from somebody else. It was grand.

Father Roy Valiquette
Rural Priest
Mt. St. Patrick

I've been in the priesthood only since 1983, previous to that I taught high school at Opeongo for years. I've been in this parish a year and a half, and I come from the Opeongo Line. This church was built in 1869 and it's one of the oldest in the valley, and the parish records go back to 1846, but the actual parish opened in 1830. This is an Irish Community — totally Irish. At one time, it was 100 per cent Irish. This parish goes as far as Dacre and Esmond and it goes towards Renfrew and then it heads towards Calabogie. It has one of the oldest graveyards, there's people buried out there going back to the 1700's. It's a fieldstone church and the stone was gotten locally. It has a hand painted fresco, a painting that is put on wet plaster, the type of thing that they would use in Europe, in Florence and Rome and so on. There are very few churches with frescos, Montreal would have them. I don't know of any in this area. An Italian artist did it. They used local girls to pose for the angels. This painting is interesting. Here you have a woman carrying a crosier. I wouldn't carry one of those. A Bishop only would carry that but here you have a woman carrying one, because in the early days women were head of the foundations of men and women. She would go to the monastery of men and women and she would carry a crosier, the same as a Bishop. The pipe organ came from Montreal. Pipe organs are getting rare in churches. There was no expense spared in the church.

Pat Lynch
Old Time Store Owner
Admaston

I guess I'm the oldest store around here, eh? Thirty-six years here, see. I got married October of 1950 and I moved here on the ninth of November. J.J. Leflare used to own it and his sister kept the store with him. So I came along and I kept after her till she finally married me, you see. She wasn't very fussy about my farm so I had to come out and buy the store from her brother. Oh, the neighbors all pitied me when I came in here. We sell a lot of soft drinks and gas and groceries and we sell a lot of clothes and straw hats and gloves and mitts. And we sell a lot of boots. We really have a good business in boots. We still heat by wood. The stove sits here and that's the stovepipe back there and we usually get it started around the first of November and right through till the middle of April. The lot was bought by Peter Ferguson in 1889 and he put up this building or store at that time, you see. I don't know what they'll do about waking me here. They should wake me back in that corner, but I'd sooner be waked up here.

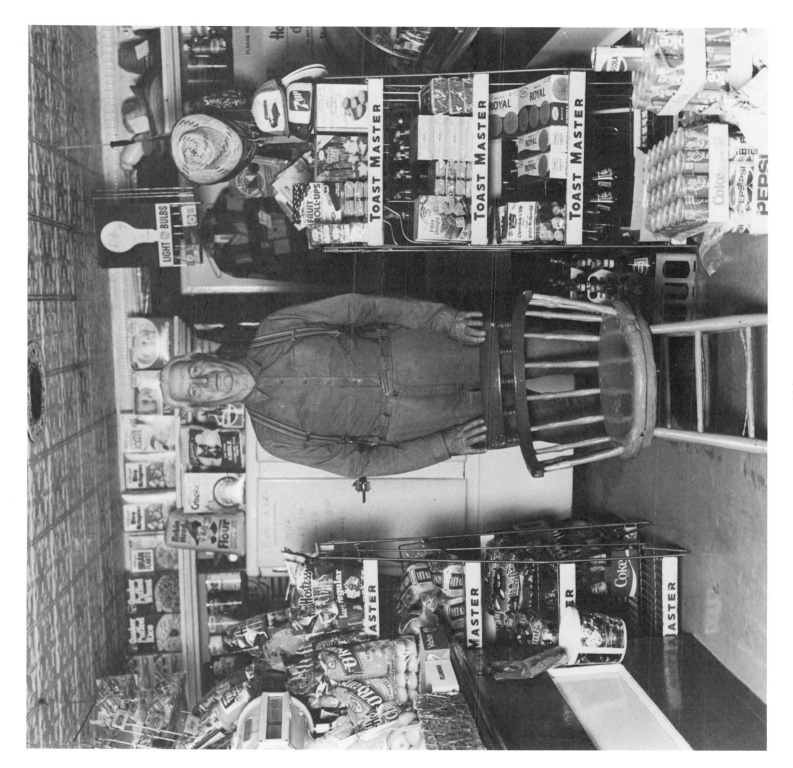

Edward Murphy
Blind Repairman
Renfrew

I've lived in Renfrew since 1944. I was in school in Brantford, a school for the blind. I went there in '19, I believe it was 1935 and up till 1943. I've been blind in one eye since I was three and it infected the other one so I gradually lost it when I was 12. I have two artificial eyes now. I bought this house in 1959. You see, I was single then and I never got married till I was 44 or 45 years old. I now repair wood stoves and I can do work on electrical stoves. I had to take the door off one because it wasn't shutting right. I do body work on fridges but actually I don't touch the mechanism part. I can drive a car but I wouldn't say how long I'd keep it on the road. When I went to school in Brantford we used to play tin can hockey every night and every Saturday and Sunday. We had our own rink at the school. We even competed one time against Detroit and they brought over their own puck with bells inside it and we were used to using a tin can. Once a tin can stops it's dead, eh, and theirs would keep rattling, eh, and we beat them 15 — 2 that night and I never forgot that. I don't miss anything. As far as seeing is concerned, people are better looking to me than they are by looking at them. I go by sound. I can tell by the sound of a guy pretty well what they're like and what their attitudes are. It's not hard to figure a person out.

Paul and Geraldine Luloff

Farming Couple
Eganville

We've been married 52 years last fall. I come from Germanicus, it's about eight miles north from here. It's a German settlement. We have one son and he lives in Germanicus. We lived on a farm all our lives. Oh, that farm, it was too rough for anything, you couldn't plow with a tractor. Too many stones. You still had to go to a lumber camp in the winter to make a few dollars. Thirty-five dollars a month cutting logs, those were good wages. We took a load of potatoes to town here one time, and sold them here for 40 cents a bag. That was a big price, 40 cents a bag. Hundred pounds in a bag. We got married in 1934. I guess I paid 30 dollars for my wedding dress. I had my suit. It was supposed to be 40 dollars, and that's the only one he had in the store, that was in Pembroke too. And he gave it to me for 20 dollars, a 40 dollar suit. We had a big celebration on our 50th wedding anniversary up at the Legion here. There was close to 300 people. People don't stay together because they marry too young. I was 30 and my wife was 22. They marry too young, that's what I figure. They don't go along a lot together to know each other real well. We went together for eight years. I knew her like a book, all I had to do was turn the pages.

John Henry McHugh

Miner
Spruce Hedge

I built this place in 1929 and I didn't live here; I was working in the mines for a number of years. I came back here in '46. I have no hydro here, I run everything by propane. They're talking about putting it in here but I don't know when. I hope they would. I'd like to see the hydro. My daughter brought those big horns in from Texas. She brought them in through the airport. She boxed them and she came in with a box about that high and I said, "What in the wide world have you got in that?" She said, "I'll show you." She came for a Christmas visit here, I guess, five years ago with those Texas Longhorns.

Cliff Langstaff
Barber
Carp

Not too many barbers around today. I don't shave people anymore. I broke my good razor and it cost too much to buy a new one. In September I'll be here 63 years. I trained in Carp, at the brick building down here. Sixty-three years ago I charged 25 cents, and shave and a haircut was 40 cents. And I had to work too. You had to shave or you didn't get any business. You had to have a good razor. It takes longer to shave you then to cut your hair. That barber pole came from Richmond and that glass come from Richmond from Pouris McBride. I got the chair and all that from him and he threw the mirror and the pole in, and that seat. In the olden days you couldn't get it tight enough. If you didn't have a haircut for Sunday you didn't go to church. Now you don't give a damn, a haircut can wait but a shave won't. I use my hair tonics very little now, just when the young lads get their hair cut. We use to get a quarter extra for them. That's what helped you, little extras. If you got a haircut and a tonic you got 50 cents. By jeez, that was all right. I worked at funeral work along with this job for 22 years. I have a old safety razor that I shaved with in the First World War. It's right down to the brass now. I shaved for the first time with a straight razor. I managed to get it off without cutting the jugular.

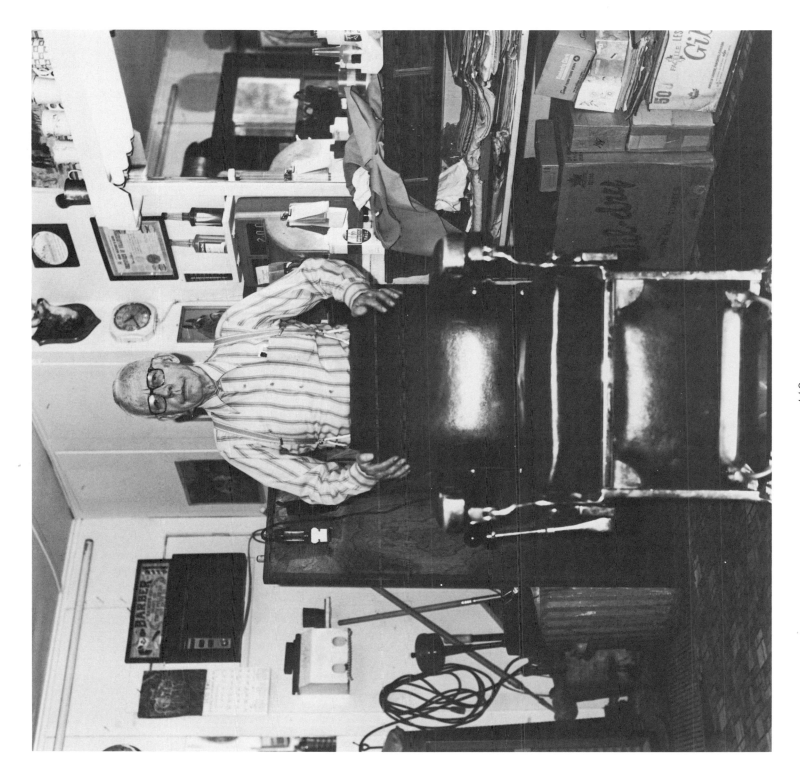

Robin Oakley
Taxidermist
Burnstown

I've been doing this for a little while, ever since I've been 16. It takes you a long time to be known. It's still pretty basic. The books I have are over a 100 years old and they come from England. My dad brought them. The first thing I ever did was a duck and it was done the old, old method and I wrapped all the body with cotton I stole out of the couch, it was a old couch. And I set it out to dry and that night the rats come and pulled the feathers out of it. I stole the eyes out of my sister's doll, bright blue ones, they were really pretty. I was experimenting. The fun of this is you get to eat everything you want and you never have to go out and hunt. I had a moose a guy brought me in and the guy cut it off at the shoulder and he gave me the whole thing from the shoulder up. I ate that all winter. That was pretty good. I get a lot of things off the highway. I see the cat catches your eye. It's the best kind of cat because you don't have to feed it. It don't do anything. Two kids came in one day and they were sitting there petting it and petting it and put it down and then went and looked around and they came back to it and picked it up again and they were petting it and all of a sudden one says, "Your cat's fake." The biggest fish I've done is a thirty-five pound muskie, and it was 60 inches, I think. It was huge and in its stomach there was three catfish and each catfish was 12 inches long. The biggest thing is that you have to make something look pretty because the wife wants to look at it too and she doesn't want some ugly thing on the wall.

Garry Vaughn
Horse Trader
Richmond

I lived about 20 years on the Fourth line. I had the ranch up there. I had 300 acres of land there. Some of it I gave away to get rid of it, about 100 acres, taken on a bet. A lot of swamp. I farmed 200 acres. The gypsies used to come. There was a blind road beside our home and they used to camp there. I remember that. It's been a while ago since there's been any gypsies. My dad used to trade horses with them. One time, we had one that wasn't very good. We wanted to get rid of it. They had a dandy. So anyway, they'd trade so my dad said, "I'll bring a set of harness and a willow tree and a chain and there's a stone there and we'll hitch him on there and if he pulls that stone then yeah, we'll trade." No, sure, this horse run loose. It didn't have a strap on him. So he mustn't been very good on the pull. I was here when the KKK came into town. There was an awful crowd there. One of those fields down there were full, down back in by Charlie Lewis' barn. I think they come from all over. I went in there at night in the fall when this fellow took off his hood, and I knew him but he didn't see me, you see, and I said, "Hello Bruce, how's it going?" He put it on real quick. I went out West with him. He was from Merrickville.

123

Christine and Florence Rice

Sisters
Perth

I got my Ph.D. from the University of Toronto. At the lab they always called me Dr. Rice but I don't usually use it. The MDs don't like you to be called a doctor. A biochemist that trained in biology can tell the doctors things that they can't figure out without the tests. I've always thought that they should work together more or less on a equal basis, and I think there are more now. They realize they've got to depend on the lab. We were born in the country. We lived out on the Second Line, and our great-grandfather came to Perth in 1815. At the Battle of Chrysler's Farm he was wounded. But anyway, he became a captain and when the war was over he was given 200 acres of land because of being a captain.

John Herlehy
A Hundred Years of Farming
Perth

I'm 100 years old. I've lived here 30 years and before I lived up on the Christie Lake Road. That's where I lived 70 years. I farmed all my life. That's my father's picture, he was killed by lightning in 1891. He was out in the field with his plow with his horses and the horses and everything were killed. I was four years old then. A lot of people ask me my secret for living so long and I tell them I didn't worry too much. I worked hard and I didn't drink and smoke too much. I never bought a pack of cigarettes in my life but I smoked cigars and a pipe. I smoked cigarettes just if they gave me one. I don't know if I would live my life over, the world has changed so much. In my day it was the horse and buggy day. I was maybe 40 or 50 years old before I saw my first car. There was a doctor who was raised on Christie Lake and we used to run out when we knew he was coming to watch the car go past. I did garden until last year. Yeah, I had a garden last year, but I had a blockage of the heart so I was down in the Civic Hospital in Ottawa and they put a pacer in. I have a violin but I never was much to play it. I used to like the old-time music. I don't like the modern music or the modern dances either. Now they just stand there and face each other.

Evelyn Moore Price

Valley Musician
Perretton

I've been organist in a little church up the road here for 53 years, and choir director for 59 years, and I was organist in Beachburg Anglican Church for some time when they were out of an organist. I got my foot in the door as music supervisor down at LaPasse. And then I taught in Beachburg and for a time up in Petawawa. I had 27 classrooms that year. And then the powers that be in Toronto sent me a wire and said, "You go. You haven't got it academically, you have it music wise." This irritated me. So I went to Algonquin College, took an aptitude test and I was into grade 11. And I graduated with my grand-daughter. I was 62 when I graduated with my grade 13. I was really proud of that. I make my living from writing and teaching. I just oozed into writing history. I had no extra training or anything. My father was a great person to keep items of history in order, and I suppose we just inherited that. My great-grandfather, William Moore, was a blacksmith and he was the first settler here and he came up from Carleton Place. It's been 59 years that I've been writing for the Pembroke Observer, not steady, but for the last 40 years it's been practically every week.

Richard Monette
Trapper
Sandy Hook

I've been filing saws for 65 years and I've been trapping since 1921. I trap mink and beaver, coon and fox and otter. I don't trap anymore; the prices were too small. I used to look after 50 or 60 traps, walked about 25 miles everyday. It's a tough life trapping. You'd leave here at five o'clock in the morning and get home at seven in the evening. I went into the bush one day and I walked a mile and a half back in here to the first trap and I had a beaver weighing 70 pounds. Well, I put him in my packsack and I came around to where I had them set, you know, and I get another one weighing 70 pounds and I put him in the packsack too and when I got within a half a mile of the truck I had another one weighing 60 pounds. Well, I couldn't get him in the packsack so I had to put a rope around him and put it over my neck and carried him under my arm. When I got to the truck, boy, I tell you, I was bushed. I never ate any of the beaver and I'll tell you why. Because, beaver, you never know when they got what they call a beaver fever. I've seen a beaver crawl out just ahead of me on shore and die but I wouldn't touch them beaver because as soon as you go and skin that, your head would swell up as same as that too. Their head would swell about that wide. Oh, there's a lot to learn on trapping there.

Nicholas and Bertha Kranz

Neighbourly Couple
Foymount

Years ago, if you wanted help you just went out and they'd come and help you. Today you have to pretty near get down on your knees and beg them. Everybody is for themself today. Years ago, you went together thrashing and sawing and all this sort of thing. Years ago, people weren't so rich; that's why they were neighbours.

Anna Dombroskie

Hardy Farmer
Wilno

I don't come from Poland. My father did. He got married in Canada. He wasn't married when he came here. You know that first war, that's the time he left there. This is my husband's house. He was born here. I lived at Round Lake. I was 20 years when I got married and I'm 87 and I've lived here since. I have no hydro, no. They didn't have hydro, the old people. His people didn't have hydro. My husband kept this farm, his father's farm, and he didn't put hydro in either. I run my TV with a battery. I still farm today. I don't feed them I just go to see them out in the yard. We have sheep and cows and horses, chickens that's all. We used to have pigs but after my husband died I let the pigs go. I didn't need them. They're lots of trouble and they take a lot of food. I can buy the meat for less. I sell eggs now. You know I bought small chickens in the spring and I got too many. I don't need all those eggs, there's too much, so I sell them. Today I have sold five dozen. They're a dollar a dozen, and that is kind of cheap but I don't need them eggs, I just as soon sell them, get rid of them. I remember I couldn't go to school. There was no school where I was brought up; there was no school, no church. We had to walk to church to Wilno, all the way from Round Lake to Wilno. We didn't go very often either, it's about 14 or 15 miles. The only thing we had to drive was horses and my father was busy all the time working on the farm and he didn't want to drive us, so we had to walk. We must of been healthy when we were young from all the walking.

Gus Risto

Woodworker

Eganville

I started doing my woodwork after I moved over here, in 1961. I done a little bit on the farm but you didn't have much chance to do it because you had to look after your cow and your horses. You had to look out for them. We lived on the farm for 35 or 37 years till we sold the farm. I bought the farm for $1,200 and I sold the farm again and took the bush out and sold it for $5,500, and I really thought if I had kept the farm for another year longer I would've got double that price. I worked awful hard but I was always pretty happy.

Alfred Keller
Cattleman
Eganville

I lived here for 24 years, and I've farmed the last 20 years or more. I grew up at Sharbot Lake, there. When I was a young lad we went to church or we went to the stores with horses, eh. We had a car but we never drove it; the roads were so frigging rough. Twelve miles to church, 16 to the closest store. Driving down there on a hot day when it was about 90° with a team of horses; you wouldn't want to go too often. You went and bought your flour and stuff in the fall, eh, because you didn't go up to the store in the winter. It was too frigging far and cold, eh. Nowadays, they dress the same in the winter as they do in the summer. They says, it's cold, it's cold. When it gets cold I put my long johns on and they stay on till it gets warm but not all the same ones. My son lives here and runs the farm now. You get no price for cattle. The meat's so gawd damn expensive in the stores. When you sell the frigging cattle you get nothing for it. But still, you get a little more for it then when I was a young lad. I remember my old man selling three year old heifers for $18 and we had to chase them for seven miles for that.

Louis Peterson
Ice Cream Entrepreneur
Almonte

I came to Canada in 1916, originally I came from Greece, when I was young, very young, I must have been about 12 years old. The worst surprise in my life was that the people couldn't talk to me in Greek. A friend of mine in Renfrew called me up one day and he says, "Just come on down and we'll start a store, a new store in Renfrew. That was the time when they had to make the ammunition in Renfrew in the war days. So everybody was busy. So I came down to Renfrew and we visited the place we were going to rent and then the owner says, "What are you going to do and how are you going to run this place?" "We're going to make candies and make ice cream and a bit of fruit," we said. "Well," she said, "You can't make candies in here." Well if we can't make candies, we can't run the store and make our own candies. So no thank you very much. So I took the train back. On the train to Ottawa I came up to the Almonte station and there was a bunch of people. And I said to myself, if all these people bought a pound of candies and an ice cream cone I'd have it made. What the hell do I want to go to Ottawa for, and I stopped. So I went to the bank manager and I said to him, "I need 500 dollars." "Well," he said, "How are you going to pay it back?" "Well," I said to him, "I'm not very far for me to come in every day and whatever I take in I bring it in everyday." He calls in his assistant there and they decided that it was all right. That was big money then. So I was buying ice cream from Ottawa. And I said to myself, What the hell is the matter with me? I can't make ice cream? I talked to myself. Well, sir, everything set so tight in my mind I couldn't sleep, I'm going to make my own ice cream. And I've been doing it ever since. I still like the vanilla better than any of the other flavours, and in the cold weather I like the chocolate.

Father John McGee

Priest and Archeologist
Osceola

I'm an archeologist by profession and I used to work at the National Museum just in the summer because I was teaching in the States at Stonehill College. That's where I got my Ph.D. I taught down there for four or five years. I got into archeology because I wanted to go to India to be a missionary and I was in Washington for about eight years and I took my theology down there at the Catholic university. I became a priest in 1940. I bought this place thirty years ago, at least. When I came back here they came to me from Opeongo school and asked me to teach there. I was teaching Latin and French and English; about five different courses. I was a teacher for years down in the States and the half-wits up here, they made you go to Toronto to the Department of Education. And they teach you nothing there, nothing at all. A complete waste of time. I was born in Osceola and my mother used to teach at a little place down here. Years ago Osceola had two sawmills and two banks and two of everything here. Even a General who lost the Battle of Mexico, he was up here living in Osceola. In those days before the railroad went through and the CPR people came up here, Cobden was a very small place and Osceola was much bigger.

Foster and Margaret Carley

Scottish Bride
Merrickville

Foster was born on a farm south of Merrickville in 1900. I was born in Ayrshire, Scotland and I came out here over 60 years ago. We came by boat, and they were all country people, all farming people. It wasn't a very big boat. We left Glasgow at 5:30 on a Friday morning and it was a week from Monday that we got to Canada. We moved right out to Carley's Corners and I was a nurse out there.

The farm where her father and her brothers moved to was just about two miles from where I was living and we met occasionally and she used to come out there for her holidays when she would get a few. And then, I guess it was the first of June in 1928, and I invited her to go to a party with me and that's where it started. From then to the next March we were married. We were married the 14th of March, 19 and 29 that's 57 years ago past. It was a happy time. There was not much grumbling like they do today.

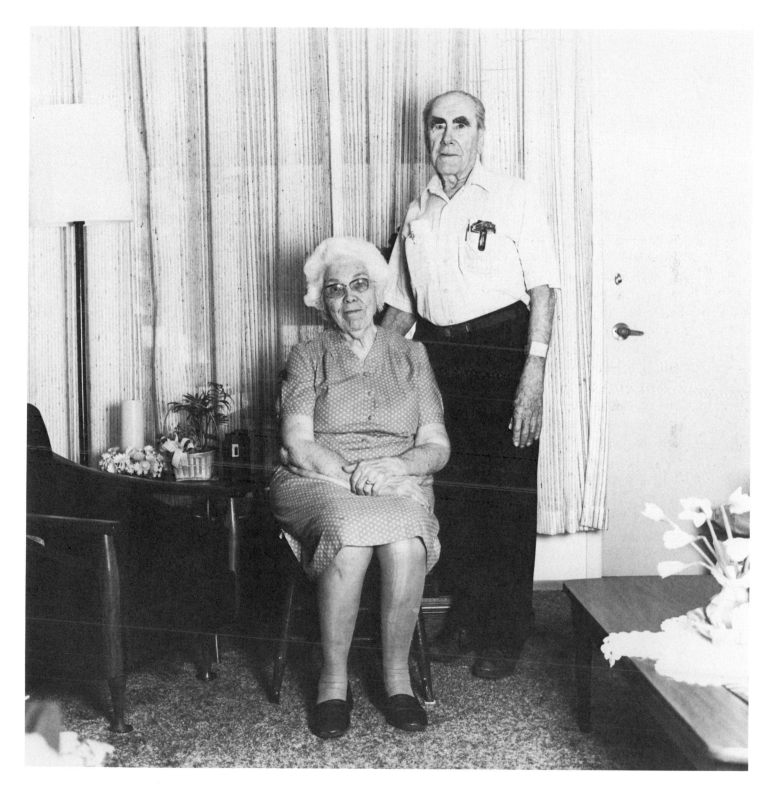

Rachel Valiquette
Homesteader
Opeongo Line

I had 14 in my family and one died in a accident. It was a funny accident. She was crossing the Lake Clear up here and a tree broke off and fell on top of her car and killed her. She never knew what happened to her. That's the only one I've lost. I never went to high school but my children had to go to Eganville to go to high school, and now they're all right. We used to have to board them in Eganville, but now there's a bus that passes every day. I'll never move into town because I got used to the country. I'll never move to town unless I have to. I was born on November the first, 1895. I'm in my 92nd year. We did lots of hard work here, not too hard, but we made a living and raised a big family — eight girls and six boys. We kept cattle, you know, and we raised grain and, well, oats and everything like that and lots of potatoes. We made our living, you know, selling logs and pines. We use to just have to take them and cut them and put them on the creek there and they drove them down to Richardson's mill and they come and bought them. He sent men in the spring. They'd come, maybe ten men, to take them down. I never was away for Christmas. They all had a nail of their own to put their socks on. We bought them everything they wanted in their socks and lots of candies and peanuts and stuff. And always presents for them. They always had a good Christmas. We always had chickens or turkeys, you know, to cook.

Gordon Bramburger

Collector
Pembroke

I collect everything, anything you want to see. There's no reason really; I just like it. I've collected everything from little items right up. When I was a young lad my pockets were full of junk. I collected marbles and chains, watch chains, jackknives, anything you want to see I put in my pocket and took them home. I never sold nothing. As soon as you sell articles you're selling your hobby. If you have two articles you'd trade with somebody else and keep the best one.

James Clemen
Old Time Fiddler
Springtown

I fiddle. Just old time stuff. Old time square dances, tunes and waltzes and stuff. No high class stuff. I don't have a favorite tune — I like them all — but my fingers are going to hell now on my left hand and that's the one you have to use. They get slow and stiff. The buggers on the right hand are as supple as they ever were. I started when I was about 12 years old and then, hell, I quit for about 20 years, then started again. I used to belong to the Renfrew County Old Time Fiddlers. I played on the stages and we've entertained in the bars and stuff. That was good. You'd go and play for a night at the bar and they'd bring you all your drinks in glasses and set them up in front of you. It helped a little, but not the next morning, hell, no. I don't know how many people live in Springtown. It's not a big place. The name is bigger than the town.

William J. Trebbien

Depression Wedding
Sebastopol Township

We've been married about 52 years. We got married up on the mountain at the Lutheran church. It was quite a big wedding and right in the Depression. We had over 100 at our wedding, I guess, and in them days the weddings weren't very big. We got an awful lot of presents but all we got in cash was three dollars. We got some pretty expensive gifts and that time there was no money but they'd go to the stores and get it on time. We have a lot of stuff yet that we got.

Gregory Kennelly
Irish Heritage
Mount St. Patrick

I was born here in 1922 and I've farmed here all my life. This was my grandfather's. My great-grandfather came out here in about 1838 from Ireland with a couple of his brothers and they wouldn't put all the family in one boat in case the boat went down. They'd divide them up. You put so many on one and so many on the next boat, and two of his brothers got on another boat and they ended up in Australia. When they were leaving home I guess they all had a few drinks until they were brave enough to say they could leave Ireland and come to a new country. It took guts to do, eh! And they were half ways across the ocean and they told them, "No you're not going to Canada, this boat's going to Australia." But when my great-grandfather came here they say he had nothing to work with. All they had was a little packsack and a couple of handspikes, and he chopped the big maples down and burned them for potash. That's what they sold for money. That's what they did in Ireland and that's what he wanted to come back in the hills for was the hardwood. They'd cut maple into the width of this table, no problem at all, and then they'd chop it up into six and eight foot chunks. That's how they originally cleaned up the land, they didn't intend to farm it; they cut the timber for the potash.

Cecil and Miriam Scharfe

60-Years Wed
Stittsville

We've been in Stittsville 51 years, I guess. I used to have a sawmill right down here and I thrashed. Name it and I've done it. We got married in 1926 and we were 60 years married on the seventh of July passed. I met her at a house party, at a dance. You don't see the like of that now, that's not modern enough. Now you have to go to a hotel. We didn't go on a honeymoon. In those days we didn't have the price of a honeymoon. No indeed, I got my honeymoon in the hayfield.

Lilly Knox
Childhood Memories
Richmond

I remember the time the school burned. That night I don't know what wakened us or what, but anyway, you could sit and read a book from the light facing us, coming into the room, it just was so brilliant. I lost all my books but one, I think it was a Latin reader. Of all the books. It just went like tinder. The school burnt in March and I think it was November they opened the other school. And there still wasn't power, there wasn't till after I got out of school. If it was a real dark day, we would go home. But the heating system never worked right in it and we would be in school and have to keep our coats on and our boots on, sometimes we'd have them on all day. Dad was a cheese maker and I was born down around Hammond, about half way between Hammond and Leonard, that's the other side of Ottawa, along the CP rail. And when I was about ten Dad sold his cheese factory and he came up to the Goodstown cheese factory, a building which is gone now, and from that he went out to Elwood to a dairy farm. Then from that he came and made cheese up the Fourth Line in the factory for a year. And from that we went down to a factory at Twin Elm and one farther down, you know where the great big slab of cement is, well that was a cheese factory. It burnt down.

John Ferguson
Actor
Renfrew

I've lived here all my life. I was born just up the road. I'm the only little one in the family. There's eight in my family and I'm the only little one. My mother had a big goiter when she was carrying me and she was drinking iodine and stuff like that to kill the goiter and it had something to do with my growth hormones. I'm in the movies, yeah. I was in the Littlest Hobo with that big dog. He pulled me out of the water. And, oh, a couple of more with Eddie Shack. They were all Canadian movies and some were showin' in the States a couple of years ago. I'm with Bizarre all the time. I made a movie called "The Brood". I seen it on television a few times. I like to see myself on TV once in awhile. I was a bellhop at the Royal York in Toronto, there. The hockey players used to stay at the Royal York and I met them all. I'd deliver light stuff and papers and stuff from the drug store and go to the liquor store. I worked there at the Royal York for 35 years and I just retired. I go back there to make my movies and with Bizarre and stuff like that. I've met a lot of movie stars too. That little guy Mickey Rooney, I sat and had a couple of drinks with him in Toronto; Bob Hope, too. And that girl that plays with Desi Arnez, Lucille Ball, I met her. Oh, I've met all the members of Parliament, I knew them all.

Albert McCoy
A Hard Life
Elphin

I was 11 and a half years old when I came to Snow Road, I didn't know a soul. I came from Clarendon. My family didn't move here, I came by myself and I went to a man's place, I never seen him before in my life. It was the 26th of January. It was a cold winter's night and, boy, I had to continue on from there doing chores. You had to do chores and work all day and go to school at the same time. I lived in the country but I wasn't used to farm work too much. Like, I could drive a single horse but I never drove a team; I learned when I got there. Sometimes you had to go out with him and fell these pine trees for logs and you standing there, and the old saw didn't work right 'cus he didn't know how to file it, and you be standing there until you were pretty well paralyzed up to the knees.

Norman Paul
Historian

Almonte

I was born in that room right over there the first of January 1900, the first day of the century and I've lived my whole life right here, and I want to die right here. I can take you back on the history of almost all the original families in this township, I can give you the history of a great many of the farms in this township, all the way back. I can remember back to 1903; I was three years old. My great-grandfather came here in 1821 from near Glasgow in Scotland. And my great-grandmother came at the same time with another family and settled on the first place down the road. The front end of this house that we're in was built in 1848 and it was remodelled in 1908 and that old house across the yard a hundred feet there, that was built for my great-grandmother in 1859. My father and my grandfather were in the lime manufacturing business. All those older buildings, stone buildings and brick buildings, the churches, schools, factories are all held together with lime that was made right here by my grandfather. And I have the old account books back in the 1850's of all the lime that was made, where it was sold, the date it was sold. I've written up all the machinery and equipment that's been on the farm right back to the cradle and the flail. And in a great many cases who it was bought from what was paid for it.

The first reaper, the first mowing machine, the first binder - all back through the last half of the century and all the way up to the present time. I've never done any research, what I know to a tremendous extent is what was handed down to me by my father's mother. I've been approached I don't know how many times, why don't I write a book? Or you just tell us and we'll write the book.

Margaret Robertson
Teacher
Burnstown

I was born in Beachburg in 1899. I came to Burnstown in 1920 to teach school. At that time it was a one room school with 36 pupils. They all walked to school, a good distance from away across the river. At that time, I got a $1,000 a year and we thought we were on easy street. Can you imagine that? I don't think I had any bad students. We had a much easier job in those days; children were very deferential. The teacher was never addressed by her first name. She was considered to be a real personality in the community. I would be asked to go and spend the night or a weekend at their homes. You can't imagine that now. They would put forward their best food and entertainment. You would get to know the children very personally. There was a much closer bond between the teacher and the pupils then, than there is now, I think. The school was a large room and all across the front were blackboards. The teacher's desk, a stark, flat-top desk was at the front, then there were four rows of seats. At the back was a big box stove that burned wood. The pipes went up and all across the room to the front and then into the flue. It had a tin jacket around it so the children wouldn't brush against it. In those days there was nothing but wool winter clothes, and they would hang their wet wool clothers over that tin jacket and you could smell wet wool all over. One Hallowe'en night some young fellows got some geese, a flock of geese that they stole some place and they put them in the school. There was no school the next day because the women took the day to clean the school. Can you imagine?

Leslie and Orpha Hanson
Compatible Couple
White Lake

I lived here 96 years, pretty much in the same house. I lived across the creek one time. They named it White Lake because of the clear water and that's the only reason. That's where it got its name from, from the Indians. The lake is 12 or 13 miles. I've skated from down there to the end of the lake and back in two hours, and that's a good while ago, I guess when I was 18, 19, 17, somewhere around there. I never was any good to remember dates. We've been married pretty near 60 years, I guess. My wife came from up around Sharbot Lake at Coxville.

I met him when he was sawing lumber in these portable sawmills. So he came up to Coxville to saw lumber and we boarded men, eh, and so that's how I got acquainted with him. He's a stubborn man. He got to have his own way, and that's right. I know, I worked with him for 58 years and I know it's got to go his way. Well, we got along together and we never fought. We have our disagreeing like that, but that's all it amounts to. I can tell my way and he can tell his way and that's it. Well, if I thought I was wrong I would quit.

Tom Sharbot
Best Damn Fiddler
Calabogie

I was born at Sharbot Lake, Ontario. It was named after my grandfather. We came from Sharbot Lake in 1914 to Calabogie. Mother lived till she was 97 and I lived with her all the time. I never got married because I had a home and a woman to keep all those years. All my life I played the fiddle. We here in the upper part of the Ottawa Valley always had some very good fiddlers, all with the traditional tunes and what not. I played what fiddling they wanted in the movie "The Best Damn Fiddler From Calabogie to Kaladar". I doubt that they'd pull it off again. You wouldn't get it going around here because they made it up in Barryvale over here in the run-down old farm places and all the old rubbish places with old abandoned cars. It was a hell of a sight and a poor thing for Calabogie. They put on two or three barn dances over here at Barryvale. We had this music and good fellows to call off a square and nice old-time round dancers and I bet ya they must of put through 35 or 40 good old-time tunes and old-time waltzes. The people thought, listen to this, this is going to be a humdinger of a movie. And say, when it came on, we never heard one tune, we never heard a bit of music, there was nothing, nothing in the line of that. They cut this all out. They just played what they wanted.

Harold Latourell

Dairy Farmer
South Gower

I've lived here for 15 years and before that we lived out that road, maybe ten miles out of South Gower, on a farm. It was a dairy farm. I was getting 65 and I couldn't farm no more and had to sell the place. I had a lot here and I moved this house here. I'd never go back to farming because I'm too gawd damn old. Jeez, I'm 81.

John McDonald

Cottage Businessman
Park Lake

I've lived here 63 years. I come here in 1924, from MacDonalds Corners. We built the first cottage here in 1938. There's a lot of people go through here. One more year after this one and we'll be in the cottage business 50 years. The beaver were extinct in this area and my great uncle, James Park, brought them back. And we had beaver ever since. Some of them cuss about it, but we've got them. They were trapped out completely. There wasn't a one left. My uncle went to the business college in Kingston for two winters. His chum was a son of the Algonquin Park superintendent and he got a little pull there and got three beaver shipped in. They were pretty near almost trapped out in the Depression in 1935. It was illegal and the season was closed but we didn't have any game warden to speak of and people trapped them and sold them. They'd get twenty dollars for a beaver pelt. They cleaned them all out. There was one colony. We watched up here on the lake and we saved them and they made a big comeback.

Thomas Wright
Old Fashioned Farmer
Pembroke

I was born right here in 1909 and I've farmed all my life. My father come here in 1900. Him and his brother settled here and then his brother dissolved and went West, so my dad took over the whole place then. I have more or less given up farming. I sold the cattle, I guess, in 1979. If I had to do it over again, I wouldn't. Not now, the present way of doing farming, I wouldn't want anything to do with it. There's too many fellows sitting in an office telling you what to do and it's all go big, go big, you know. I farmed with horses right up till I got the tractors. No, it was later than that. I had horses after I had the tractor, too. I think it was '56 I sold off the last horse.

Howard McNeely

Auctioneer and Barber
Carleton Place

When I was going to school, I always enjoyed people. I love people. I decided to be a barber because in the barbershop you meet so many people. I was going to go to school to be a barber and some of the older barbers told me that it would be better to learn right in the barbershop. I trained with another barber. When you first go in you don't get up to work on the customer, you stropped razors, sharpened scissors and kept the barbershop in good shape and you became naturalized to people. This very, very good friend of my father's came in and he says to me, "What are you doing in here?" And I said, "I'm going to learn the barbering trade." And he said, "You'll never learn it sitting there, get up here and cut my hair." So, right or wrong, I had to get up and I said to the barber that was training me, "Will I?" He said, "Well, that's between you and him." So I got up and cut his hair. I don't know if you called it cutting, it was shorter. I said to the barber, you better come over and staighten this out. And he said, "No, no, this is a barber here; he cut my hair and from now on he's to cut my hair." And every time that lad came in, I cut his hair. That's about the way I got started. Boys' mothers always wanted it short and they'd come in and they'd get the young lad up in the chair and they'd sit behind them and you would say, "How does he want his hair cut?" They's put their fingers like this: short, short, low so that he couldn't hear. And I've seen them lads cry, go out of this shop just crying and I'd be scared that they'd run across the road and get killed. Their mothers would get down out of the chair and they'd spank them and put them back up. And that's no fooling.

Herschel Reilly

A Drop of Royal Blood
Richmond

The Duke of Richmond came and spent a night over there. That's where our grandfather lived. That's where my mother was born. My mother's grandmother was Lady Anne Copeland. I don't say the little drop of blood is getting down pretty thin. There's a little drop of royal blood in there, my mother's mother. Did you ever see the book "The Woman From Ireland"? Well, you get all the history out of that. That woman from Ireland is our great-great-grandmother. We knew that this young officer, Sgt. Vaughan, was over during the revolution over there, and on his way back these Copelands were on the ship and fleeing from Ireland and she was this young girl of about 16 and he was a young officer and he fell in love with her and wanted to marry her. Her mother wouldn't allow it at that time, a girl of that age to marry. So Mother used to tell us the story of sitting on her grandmother's knee and her telling her all this. But we never knew really if ever they had eloped or if they had got married in a church. But a friend was out and now it's down in the only cathedral in Quebec City. It's on the wall in the cathedral there where they were married in that old church. They blazed their way through the bush and this is where they settled. Once Grandfather Vaughan was walking to Perth for flour and he left Grandmother with three or four small children. At this time her mother came as far as Quebec City but she never came on, and Grandmother was afraid that her mother would come on and see what she was living in, just a few logs. When she came she thought she was coming to a nice new home here. When she came there was no roof on it and there was a few logs closed in some way. Anyway, when he was leaving he warned Grandmother to keep on a fire to keep the wolves away. So she kept, with the children, piling on brush to keep the fire going and the more fire they put on the more the wolves howled. They were scared stiff, but it was the owls coming to the light.

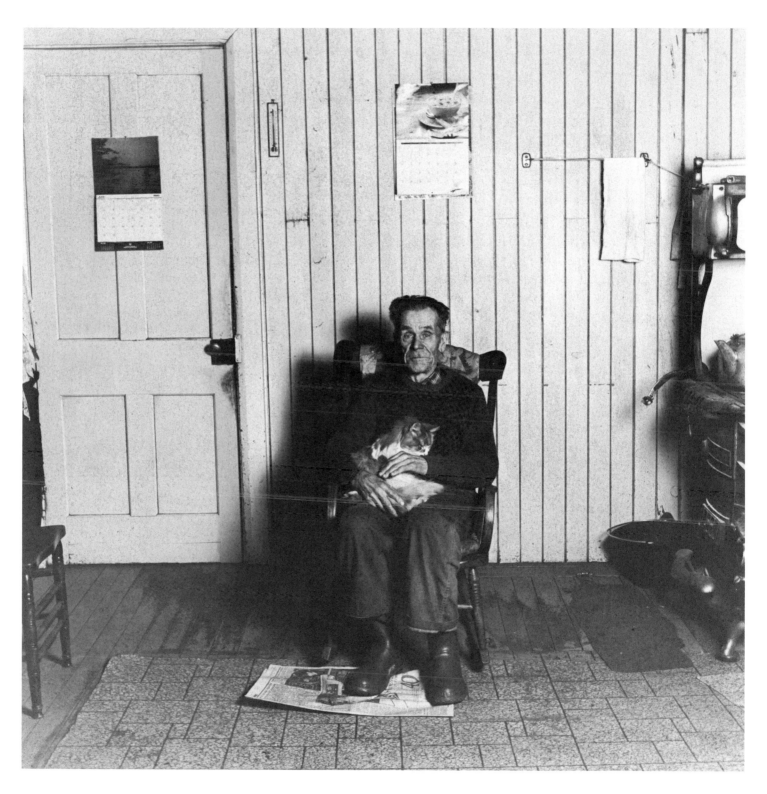

Allan Kasmack
Township Clerk
Foymount

When I was 20 years old, I took the job of being treasurer in the school, in a country school. It was only one school and there was only about 20 children in the school. There was five schools in the township and each one had a school board. That was too much work, so they formed the Sebastopol Township school area and they appointed me as secretary treasurer of five schools. And then about a year or two after, they were in trouble with the township here so I took the job of township treasurer and clerk and I was township clerk and treasurer for 30 years. And I had to farm besides. We didn't farm as big as the lads do now but we had 65 or 70 head of cattle. And on top of that, I bought a big machine and I got it sent from Saskatoon, in fact, and I took the contract to plow the roads for five years. After five years I gave it up, but after that we had plowed roads. So I was sort of busy. We started out 100 years ago with 100 acres and today we have 1,300.

The Burke Brothers
Gentlemen Bachelors
Maberly

We never got married; any of us. We could of got married but we never got around to it. When we were young we didn't have too much money, and when we got the money we didn't want to get married, didn't want to divide it up. No, we just kept working away. I'm the youngest and I'll be 67 and my name is Stewart. The next is Cecil and he's 73, and Edwin he's 75. I came here when I was seven months old. You know, it's nice country here, not good farming country, but it's nice country to live in. There'll be never any place I'll be happier than here. It's a nice place here. We have no Hydro. We're happy the way we are, the way it is. We'd have to get a fridge and stove. We don't farm a lot since we sold the other farm. We cleared 340, we used to have a 1,000 acres and we sold our upper farm in Sherbrooke, eh. We have 12 head of cattle and four big horses. We like the heavy draft horses. I'd go a mile to see a nice heavy draft team harness. Just my glory.

Art and Elsa Stewart
Community Supporters
Pakenham

Elsa came from Renfrew and I came from just near Renfrew at Goshen. We met each other in Guelph, at University there. We did quite a lot of work in redeveloping the village here back 20 years ago. A lot of old buildings we bought and refurbished them. We developed the Centennial Restaurant down here, it was our Centennial project. We built Stewart House and lived there for quite a while, then it was turned over to the United Church and is operated now by a committee of the Ottawa and Renfrew United Church. There's a group of Buddhists in down there, it's the first time we have ever had them. We developed it as a community centre for group study and education. We've travelled a great deal. We were in Westminster Abbey for the Coronation of Queen Elizabeth. We were there from the Canadian Federation of Agriculture. The president was a bachelor and he had a invitation but they didn't accept anybody who weren't couples, so he gave us his credentials. It was quite an experience. We both received recognition as members of the Order of Canada. It's one of the top things in Canada.

Barney McCaffrey
Musician
Wilno

We came up to the area in '69. We came essentially from Peru. We were two years in Peru as volunteers. I make my living by a little of this and a little of that. The farm supplies us with 80 per cent of our food. The soil is very poor. We planted a bunch of Christmas trees and about 50 per cent of them might have survived and that's just pines. That's how poor it is. We've been building up the gardens ever since we moved out with manure. We do everything organically. I'm also a teacher and a calligrapher and we sell some produce from the farm. For 16 years we had the community school of Killaloe, which was a home-centered school, co-operative, parent run. Right now we're in another home-centered school because we couldn't keep ours going. After our kids graduated, there just weren't enough other kids. We have to have five to keep a school going. I play everything but hard rock. I just can't play it. I'm keyboards, mainly accordion, piano, a little guitar but mostly acoustic type guitar. I sing in 21 languages, I just did a couple of nights of Irish songs on St. Patrick weekend, I know over 60 Irish songs and written a couple myself and collected Valley music. We played about 12 years ago over at a dance hall just south of Barry's Bay. It used to be called The Hog Wrastler. The guys would come out of the bush on a Saturday night and go have a fight. We could sense this tenseness in the air. The dance went over very well, but as soon as the dance was over, we got everybody out of the hall. We looked out on the lawn and there's like 20 guys all rolling around on the lawn, fighting like crazy, like they've just been itching to do that all night long, you know, because that's what they used to do.

Annie Steffan

Pioneering Family
Barry's Bay

I was born here in 1916. I was married 50 years in '82 and my husband died after that. I lived on the next farm here and my husband worked in Quebec when he'd come and visit me. And then he come and we got married in '32. I was only 16. He was 20 years older then me. I had 16 children. We had a hard time. When I was a young girl I worked for my father in the bush, cooking for him too, bake the bread. I was 12 years old and I skidded the logs and took care of the horses; had two horses. When I was a young girl at the farm I had to milk while my mother was to go as a nurse to some people and visit all the people. She delivered 200 children, I think, by herself. Every woman got her to get the baby. There was no doctors, no nurses, none around. And she'd go away and I was nine years old and I have to stay at home and I milk nine cows and separated the milk for my mother. When my father worked on the road I had to work in the field for him all the time. Two horses I had to hitch to a big wagon and to get the oats and all the grain from the field to the barn. It was a poor time, very poor. My two brothers can play fiddles and me and my brother Eddie can play accordion. I sing but Polish songs. A lot of Polish people play the accordian.

Mary McHugh and Kevin McHugh

Roughin' It
Spruce Hedge

I've lived here all my life. I'm 84. I can't get around very fast. We farmed when my brother was living but we quit that. I never was married. This is my nephew. He is my brother's son, and it's just the two of us out here. The house is 125 years, if not more. There's four generations here now. This house was put up with an axe, nothing else, and a hammer. You look out there; the logs are that width. My grandfather built it. They came over from Ireland. I'm Irish to the core. It's nice and quiet up here. We never wanted for anything. The work was hard, but it was honest. We have a cousin who lives up here in the summertime and he has a car and he brings our groceries. We phone into the store and I order it and he picks it up. When he's not here, I hire a taxi. That's a sweet tune — 14 dollars each way. There isn't much for the clergy on Sunday, eh, if you put out 28 dollars for a taxi. I never go near the telephone unless somebody calls me. It's nice for emergencies and to call the store. I haven't got electricity. I've got a generator. I've got the house wired but we never use it. We use the coal oil lamps. This time of year you hardly use your lights, you know. It's pretty near bedtime when daylight's over.

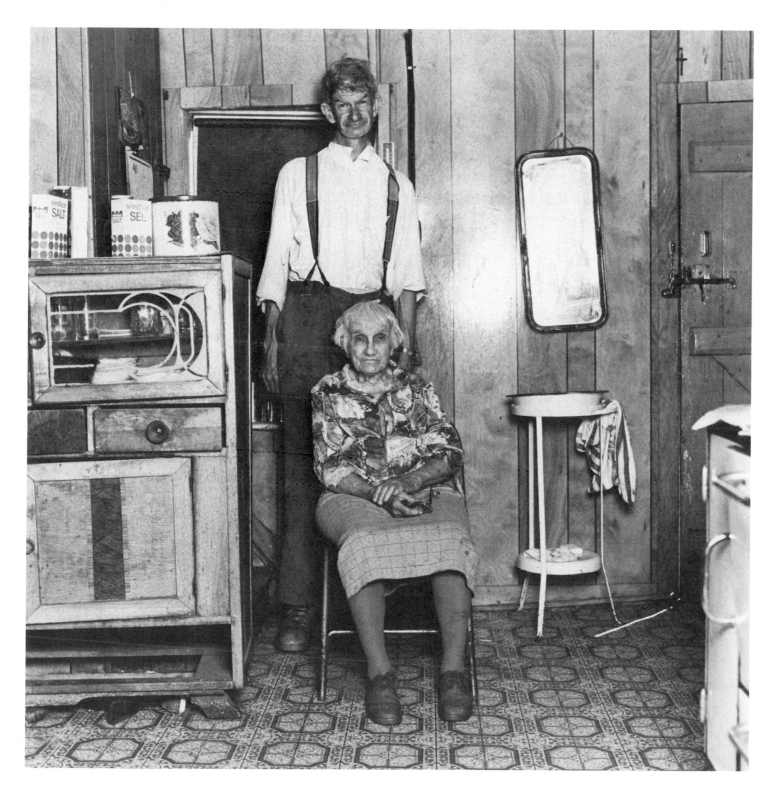